A LIFETIME OF WEALTH –
AND HOW NOT TO LOSE IT

**Exploring the sudden- and
not-so-sudden wealth events
we can experience in life due to**

- o **Business sale/succession**
- o **Pension options for life**
- o **Inheritance from family**
- o **Lottery or other winnings**

**Securing lifestyle, life-values, life-income
and an estate to endear your name forever.**

If we could miss the gravest errors

that have robbed people of their wealth

and find how to enjoy the strongest results to

perpetuate the wealth we build & receive in life

HOW AWESOME WOULD THAT BE!

A LIFETIME OF WEALTH –

AND HOW NOT TO LOSE IT

Brian Weatherdon
MA, CFP, CLU, CPCA, MDRT.

ISBN 978-1489579546

Author: Brian Weatherdon, Burlington Ontario, Canada.
Editor: Craig Harris, Edit Insight Ltd. Ontario, Canada.

Note: views expressed are those of the author alone and do not necessarily reflect the financial firms and product manufacturers he represents.

Contents

Chapter 6 - Conclusion

Appendix

Acknowledgements

"Too many to name" is a phrase that comes to mind, for we are all so very dependent on those who have gone before, and those who support our endeavours today.

My parents indelibly shaped my values and perspectives on life, giving, sharing, and creating a better world. My father's role as a life insurance advisor, returning from management into personal service, certainly provided the lines within which I explore my own life and career. My brother (deceased 1979) and sister also cultivated my persistence and resilience to keep creating something better – and have fun in the task.

My wife Virginia and children are a total joy to me. I admire their strengths, each one of them. My earlier career in Christian ministry, during graduate studies 1979-1982 and as an ordained minister 1982-1995 connected me so deeply with the lives, struggles, achievements and journeys of several thousand people. Their stories continue in my heart and within my own journey as I serve people today.

My community is rich and vibrant, exposing me to the development of business, social infrastructure, philanthropy, and of course family life where we each seek to enjoy our journeys, our family, our ongoing opportunities to create and savour the lives we enjoy.

My business and personal life is blessed indeed with our superb and dedicated staff at Sovereign Wealth Management Inc. of Burlington Ontario, and my dear and lasting friend (and principal of our firm) Whitney Hammond.

I acknowledge also the exemplary stories, courage and self-less leadership of fellow-members of the Million Dollar Round Table, the pre-eminent organization of insurance- and financial-advisors representing the service of our industry in over 100 countries of the world. Without MDRT our world would be poorer, our future less abundant, our families less secure, our own personal visions less vibrant, our businesses less stable, our estates less generous, our philanthropy less miraculous! To my personal MDRT friends and 35,000 other advisors world-wide whom I know less well, I gratefully salute you and contribute this volume to our combined resources in serving our clients with excellence.

I thank financial advisors who will use this book and/or the associated website, www.GuaranteedIncome4Life.ca as a resource to aid their own client conversations. I want nothing more than to support stronger results for our respective clients. All too easy it is to lose money: as financial advisors we want to help our clients preserve their financial resources and enjoy the life they choose, while protecting the richest advantages for their families and community. I salute you, and welcome you to consider joining if you're not yet a MDRT member.

To Craig Harris who kindly has edited this volume and become my friend during this work, I also give my sincere and heartfelt thanks. While any faults are my own and I am solely responsible for them, Craig helped finalize the order and smooth the text to be as readable and usable as possible. Craig was formerly editor of Advocis' FORUM magazine for insurance- and financial-advisors in Canada. Most sincere thanks to you Craig!

I believe in professional collaboration as Stewards of the future we help protect and create. To my friends and trusted colleagues in law, accounting, and various other business services, you have my utmost respect today and always, because serving together we can offer lasting stewardship of our clients' lives and resources.

Now or soon, you can visit www.GuaranteedIncome4Life.ca to join an ongoing community discussion on the subjects in this book. I look forward to seeing you and hearing from you there!

BW

"Do not brood or bottle things up, problems don't disappear, they have to be worked on and worked out"

"Most of us will not choose how we will die, but we all choose – every day – how we will live"

Peter Legge, The Runway of Life, 2005

About the author

There was a time when I knew embarrassingly little about money. In 1987, I was a minister in Nova Scotia, attending a gym with a friend who would check his stock reports in the newspaper to learn if he was comfortable buying lunch that day. It intrigued me and set me on a vast inquiry about money – how wealth works, what happens when illness or death hits a young family, why an 83 year old could die of stress from running out of money. My curiosity grew and I borrowed books widely by inter-library loan (no *Google back then*). That is what started my passion to help create financial security for families, individuals and communities.

An example occurred (*before entering financial service in 1995*) when I visited a gentleman 72 years of age. As I entered the home he mentioned he had 32 months to live. I was confused how he would know this. He replied: "You saw the for-sale sign on the front lawn. When the house sells, I'll move into the lodge with my wife. In 32 months we'll have to die because the money will be gone!"

Such experiences weighed on my heart. As a pastor in various communities from 1979 to 1995, I had often found that our financial world was failing to protect people and resolve the urgent problems that arise in their lives. I wanted to learn how we could protect families, sustain seniors' financial security and ensure people have resources to enjoy life as long as they live. This became an absolute passion for me, and it continues to direct my focus to provide a lifetime of financial security.

In 2001, I frequented stores seeking a book on lifestyle financial planning. I assumed someone would have written such a book, and I wanted to give copies away for education. This exercise was in vain; no such book was available. The books instead focused on financial products, arguing why this or that approach to investing or insurance, tax and properties would serve the reader. Nothing seemed to focus on aligning wealth, financial planning and lifestyle. In other words, the books were focused on financial details rather than life results.

In the years since, I've developed my own theme of "Lifestyle Financial Planning." If you ask me today what I do, I answer: "I help people align their wealth with the life dreams (and future estate) they want to enjoy." This translates into a simple and clear message: "It's the financial process of life decisions to achieve your goals and enjoy the journey."

Thank you for joining me on this journey. Thank you for sharing your journey with others!

Yours in Financial Security for Life!

Brian Weatherdon

Introduction

You're opening this book because you want answers about money. How can wealth serve you today and in the future? For some, this question arises from owning a business. For others, it involves decisions around a pension. Some may visit here because they have received an inheritance. Others may have benefited from an unexpected windfall, such as a lottery.

This book is designed for all of you and the unique situations you face. It's easy to see you won't need to read all of it; focus on the areas most related to your own questions. The last chapter will explore the key financial mistakes to avoid and approaches to help you safeguard your wealth. I trust this book will give you the answers to what you're seeking.

Pensions are the first section of the book. You've had a career in business, or perhaps in health or teaching in a university, and you're approaching retirement. The pension decision initially seems like a simple choice – a guaranteed allowance versus a more flexible, personalized income to fit your lifestyle and estate planning needs. We'll explore many features of this decision so you understand the options and feel comfortable with the right choice for you. At times, I will bluntly tell people to stay in the traditional pension! Yet we'll also explore situations where you'd choose to "take the money and run" if this better aligns with how you want to enjoy life. You'll be surprised at the impact this choice can have for you in unlocking new opportunities for you and your family.

Business is the second section of this book. Your business is ultimately a "wealth business" because it is the foundation of financial security for you, your family and possibly future generations. We'll explore how you feel about health and lifestyle, personal identity and family dynamics – even before you put your business on the market. We'll consider preparing for succession or sale within family, to staff or to outsider buyers. Many business owners are focused on the "here and now" of planning. However, the ultimate goal of your business should be to unlock and collect the greatest value to fully support your life dreams and goals.

Inheritance is a wealth event that many people will be experiencing in the coming decades. This isn't just about receiving money – it's also about the feelings you may experience and the responsibility that comes with this money. It encompasses knowing the giver(s) and realizing how "values" and "wealth" can forge a companionship to insulate you from risk and protect you from loss.

Lottery and other winnings, while a dream for many, are a fourth kind of wealth event. These can suddenly – ready or not – put a great deal of money into peoples' hands. Yet it's sad: winners too often become losers. That's why you should be reading this section. If you're serious about protecting this windfall, the first step is to explore how sudden wealth is associated with deeper values and what you want your life to become.

Avoiding the greatest financial mistakes is our next destination. Does anyone feel their wealth came to them so quickly and easily that losing it doesn't matter? Would you willingly put it all at risk? Surely you say "no!" But mistakes happen. People lose money every day; some families have lost in days what it took decades to build. How? They didn't know what mistakes to avoid. Advisors took risks their clients didn't understand. Or they were victims of fraud. If the greatest risk is "not knowing what we don't know," then this section can show:

(i)   how to build a vault around your wealth; and

(ii)   how to create the life-value and enjoyment you want for yourself and others.

Sharing this discussion with others is vital too. I'm not giving you this book to hide and use it only for yourself. Share it with key family members. Share it with trusted advisors. If you're an advisor, give this book to your clients and tell them to write down their notes and bring these back into their discussion with you. Advisors can reach me for further information; I'm grateful to put our minds together to create stronger results for everyone. If you're lacking an advisor, I can share how one selects a professional advisor to strengthen the team that will support and secure your future.

1st Bonus: Building your Future Dream is a section on developing, clarifying and realizing your future dream. This is a whole-body experience I call "visioning" – it stimulates all our senses to get the creative juices going.   If life's treadmill kept you too busy to imagine the future, a story of someone else's experience might light the path for you.

2nd Bonus: Create *Your* Plan.   The financial planning process is vital to your success and satisfaction. Every institution will take deposits; too few, however, will listen, engage you and help in the creation of a customized financial plan. So here I offer examples of a formal process used in our own firm, and an experiential viewpoint in which my clients have described the personal impact of this service.   Planning to secure your life and wealth must be a thorough and clear process to assure sustainable results.

3rd Bonus: 20 ways to Brainstorm your Future. Use pen and paper, or brush and canvas if you prefer, to open the channels toward the life and purpose you want to be enjoying.

Note: all references to people and places have been changed, and stories in composite form help elicit potential learning experiences for the reader while taking the least space to do so. We have eliminated technical terminology and acronyms that would refer to specific products or to tax- and legal-arrangements specific to a given region or country.   What's missing in this regard can be fully compensated by working with an accredited advisor or group to help you establish the results you seek and means of attaining them where you reside. We'll refer to this again and specifically in the context of your professional "stewardship team" and the value of their service in securing your future.

Chapter 1

DECISIONS FOR YOUR PENSION

Welcome to this section to consider your choices about your pension plan. If you're nearing retirement and want to see the future more clearly, this section will be very helpful.

If you're keen on staying in a pension plan, I'll probably suggest you consider the other view. And if you're aching to get the money out of your pension so you manage it yourself (or even with help), I'll stress the need to weigh this decision carefully.

The fact is you have a choice of how to draw the value accumulating in your pension plan. You need to examine all the options. What are the possible risks if you live too long or too short? What could you lose in health benefits? How will you cope with inflation? What is the possible impact for your spouse? What is the long-term effect on your family in event of illness or emergencies? What difference would it make for your estate or your charitable goals?

Other personal considerations relate to how you see your future? Do you plan to continue working or to retire fully? Would you hazard to put your pension eggs into a new business development? In terms of personal spending, would it be best to retire on a fixed allowance for life? Or instead would you prefer to gain flexibility to "live larger" in the early years and adjust your income to suit your energy and desired expenditures?

These are vital questions to keep in mind as we survey the following sections and the accompanying stories. The most important insights here will be those that relate to your own circumstances and how you want to enjoy life!

1. Choosing What to Do with your Pension Plan

You have a defined-benefit pension plan. You are likely at a point in your life of researching options and deciding how to maximize this value for yourself and your family.

What are your pension plan choices?

1. One choice is to draw a fixed income from the pension plan for the rest of your life. This may be a set monthly income or a reduced-income that continues further payments to your spouse if you were to die first. The pension administrator can give you a summary of these options. If it's not clear, ask the administrator for a more detailed explanation or get a financial professional to review these options with you.

2. The other main choice is to "commute" the pension. This simply means either receiving a taxable lump sum of money or allocating the funds directly into a personal tax-sheltered account for retirement savings or income. The pension administrator can explain if you have this choice, or if this is an option you could exercise only up to a given age. Assuming you can commute, the value of this money will be in the report from the pension administrator.

These are real-life options facing many people approaching retirement. A business professor recently shared with me that most of his colleagues are commuting their pension upon retirement. Two things about this were notable to me. First, I couldn't believe that his colleagues en masse would be commuting a pension in which the inflation indexing is currently guaranteed up to 8% (plus catch-up if inflation exceeded 8%). This is a rich plan; why would anybody leave? The second notable issue is what level of information and education the colleagues had before making this decision. I was also told that many of his colleagues who commuted their pension realized a few years later that it was a mistake. You and I know that avoiding such a "mistake" is why we're having this discussion.

So, how do you decide?

The first decision is to confirm with your pension administrator or human resources department whether you have the choice to commute, and what time limits or other requirements might be involved.

Second, you'll want to consider the benefits on either side of this choice. Perhaps you want the security that a fixed-format of income is destined to be paid every month for the rest of your life. Such comfort can mean everything! On the other hand, there is the freedom to align your income with lifestyle enjoyment. This might mean doubling up your income in the earliest years, seeding a new business that will create a new stream of income – or bequeathing your pension value to family and grandchildren.

A specific consideration may be your health. If you have serious illness or ongoing health concerns, a prime issue may be how to choose the best value for your family.

Another issue is the health of the pension plan itself. A shocking number of pension plans are underfunded. As we'll see, it can become very difficult for trustees to make up the underfunding, meaning that the pension may be forced to pay less than its promised benefits. Unless a pension is well above average, there could be future decisions that drop pension benefits by 20% to 50% (even to existing retirees at that time). I think of this when I see people in their 70s working in department stores and fast-food restaurants; I wonder how many of them were forced back to work because of an underfunded pension. We'll explore all these themes as we move forward.

2. Lifestyle and its Impact on your Pension Choices

One of the reasons people are talking about commuting pensions is the appeal of the freedom it can offer. The flip side is the possible security of a flat or fixed-income pension. I like to frame this discussion in terms of how you want to enjoy your life, in the context of the changes on your horizon. You can view your retirement as three distinct time periods with varying goals and spending patterns.

Earlier years of retirement are often when we expect to be most active. You may want to see and do many things at this period. You can travel widely, engage in sports and new activities, get a new degree in university, help with family and community. You're limited only by your interests and imagination. Accordingly, people tend to spend more money in this season of life.

Middle years of retirement begin whenever you decide they begin. You might be 73 or 85 but typically the time comes when we tend to become more sedentary, travel less widely, incur fewer expenses and require less income.

Later years of retirement may bring the onset of chronic health or mobility issues that restrict travel and other activities. This is also the time of increased costs for supported living and health care.

How will your vision of life and your dreams of future lifestyle influence your pension choices? Some stories we'll touch on later include Eric, who left teaching to do part-time consulting and gain flexibility to care for his wife. Pat commuted her pension and turned much of it into seed capital for a business to sell later as a larger nest egg. You perhaps want to walk into the screen of your own movie, live and write the script day-by-day as you choose, aligning your pension choices to fully support your lifestyle. A pension decision then is about more than money; it is really about life and the spending patterns to enjoy your dreams.

3. What About the 60% Rule? Do You Want a Better Deal?

Traditionally, the standard pension plan may offer a 60% survivor's pension to your spouse. The survivor pension may range from 50% to 80%, depending on the plan and the options you choose when you elect to remain with the plan. The point – a spouse typically will receive much lower monthly income if the pensioner dies.

If we look at traditional pension plans, this is how our parents might have experienced their retirement income. The pension may have come from government, a manufacturer, a bank . . . wherever our parents worked. And so naturally we're familiar that if dad passed away at 70, mom continued to receive a fraction of dad's pension. However, would you possibly like a better deal for surviving family members?

Marie's story is worth reading. She was in her 50s when she told me that no woman in her family had ever lived to 65. She was retiring early so she could enjoy family and other experiences, as she was worried her years might be cut short. Unfortunately, her husband had been chronically ill and Marie figured neither of them was destined to get full value out of a standard pension plan. Given Marie's circumstances, she chose to commute her pension. Not only did it offer more flexibility for income while she was living, it also offered full continuing income for her husband if he would survive her, and thus assist with expenses of his ongoing care. As a bonus, the remaining value at death would benefit their estate, and they specified this as a financial gift and ongoing 'love-letter' to their grandchildren. This personalized pension plan helped Marie bypass the 60% rule and creatively express her ongoing love and support for her family!

A very different situation could arise if you don't even need the money. Consider if your family income from all sources will be more than enough to supply your lifestyle needs. Would it be better to accept a fixed monthly allowance with 60% remaining to the surviving and sole taxpayer at the highest marginal tax rates? Or could you consider personalized strategies to support your family, and perhaps make a major impact to charity, both while living and through your estate? Raising such a question opens the door to maximizing planned gifts for your family and community, as well as advanced tax planning.

Most people's greatest concern will be their own life income – how to secure sufficient spending power for the rest of your life. Depending on circumstances, many will choose a level of assurance that comes with a pension plan offering 60% continuing income for a surviving spouse. In other cases, you may want your spouse's personal and health circumstances to find greater financial support.

4. What is the Trustee's Perspective?

If you're making a major financial decision, wouldn't it be valuable to know who's on the other side? What is their perspective on the choice you're about to make? We often assume pension trustees want to keep the pension assets under their own management, supposing that "bigger is better." But trustees might not always take this position.

I don't envy pension trustees for a moment because they are in a very tight spot these days. Consider how these trustees are paying increasing sums of money to retirees during a time of historically low interest rates, wobbly investment markets and underfunded pension plans. It sounds like a dangerous position. So do you suppose you'd accept the responsibility of a pension trustee?

Your mission, if you choose to accept it, is to continue paying out retirement pensions even though:

- Interest rates are at historically low levels;

- Bonds are paying <3% guaranteed even for 30 years, and may sustain capital losses when interest rates start to rise;

- Stocks are limited to 50% or 60% of the portfolio to reduce market risks, yet markets can fall precipitously as in 2008 and devastate returns in pension plans; and

- People are living longer; in fact, the fastest growing segment of the population is the >85 group.

These factors combine to threaten what pension trustees can accomplish today. And the pressure is not going away. A key solution will be getting more funding from business or the government – an unlikely option in difficult economic times. This issue is not going away in our generation.

Logically, some pension trustees would look at the decision to the commute and take the value of your pension as lifting a liability off the books of the pension fund. Ongoing risks – investment, demographics, longevity – may be lower for trustees as people personalize their pension arrangements.

Remember, however, that if you commute your pension, the trustees will lose the death benefit they would have traditionally received when you pass away. Since you've moved the money from the pension plan, trustees have no access to it for other pensioners. This, of course, is because your pension value became your personal asset, and thus a value to your own family.

5. Does your Decision Impact your Health, Dental and Travel Insurance?

Staying in a pension plan might offer some level of continued health insurance. In many cases, you would want to protect such insurance if it can continue. However, there are other solutions for health benefits. Caution is clearly important in making these decisions. The best time to compare your options is well in advance of any pension decisions.

There can be many ways to access health benefits when you're retiring. For example:

- You may convert your existing benefits plan into a private coverage;
- You may be able to participate in benefits of a professional association or retired teacher pension plan;
- You could apply for private coverage designed for the benefits you want; or
- Your spouse may have continuing benefits so you don't need your own.

Continuing health insurance upon retirement will generally be different than what you've had up until now. Here are some of the questions to consider.

- Do you need to know how existing medications will be covered?
- Is there a pre-existing illness that could threaten your coverage?
- Is there a modest ongoing condition that an insurer could reject?
- Will you be out-of-country for extended periods?

Sometimes your best option may be staying in the pension plan to maintain the right to continued insurance coverage (in situations where this is still available). Following are some of the questions you can raise to help make a sound decision.

- What value can you determine/calculate with this coverage?
- How long can you be assured of it continuing?
- What is the cost-sharing arrangement – if any?
- How much control would you have someday if they increased charges, made you pay a greater share of the costs, reduced reimbursements or stopped the plan altogether?

Too often, these questions are ignored and people make decisions that are not in their best interests. Breaking down continuing health and dental benefits in your pension (and your spouse's pension) and examining private options can help clarify your choices. This will put you in a position to choose the option that is right for your individual circumstances.

6. What Advisory Support Will You Need?

Let's say you saved a large sum of money, perhaps $250,000 or more, in retirement savings, and you're holding this money with some kind of financial institution or advisor. If you choose to stay in your pension plan, is there any reason why you would consider changing your financial advisor? That is unlikely because this person has probably earned your trust and loyalty. Regardless of the pension decisions you face, there is likely no reason to change your advisor.

If you're planning on building a personalized pension plan, that is a different scenario. The value coming into your hands will likely dwarf anything you've invested up to now. You may want to reconsider whether the institution or advisor you've been working with on previous assets is fully suited to manage this higher sum and the processes needed to create a secure life income. Ask yourself: how capable do you need this team to be and who is going to do this kind of work for you?

As an advisor, I know you need financial security for life. This means risk-avoidance strategies need to be developed and implemented. We need to honour the goals for your personalized pension as long as you live – and for the estate value for your immediate family and ensuing generations. It's often the case that the type of advisor and team you require for this kind of service is different than what you have had in the past. If your future is going to be more complex because of your greater wealth, it's vital to get a clear and safe strategy to protect life income and estate values.

7. Fixed or Flexible Income for the Rest of your Life?

Earlier, we discussed lifestyle choices. Let's revisit this because it is one of the most misunderstood factors of retirement. Life isn't a straight line after we retire. And it isn't just one final period of life before "kicking the bucket." We know intuitively through our own experience, but also through a few decades of studying the aging process that retirement years are divided into three (or perhaps even four or five) sections.

There's early retirement; the first time period of your retirement, lasting anywhere from 8 to 15 years. Here, we can live vigorously, youthfully, and cheat the calendar while checking off the experiences we most want to enjoy in those early years.

Then there comes a time we might describe as more sedentary. During this period, people are traveling less, perhaps to Florida instead of Europe, hiking trails near home instead of the West Coast Trail or Patagonia. This is a mid-period of retirement, possibly itself divided into sections due to health, family or other factors.

A third major horizon eventually comes when we're not as strong or healthy as we used to be. This is when our health costs increase the most and support in our own home, or in "a home," can become necessary. In fact, 85% of a person's health costs will occur in the last 5 years of life. Looking forward, we know governments are reducing responsibility for health, cutting exposure to the enormous health cost of an aging population. So it will fall onto our own shoulders, or that of our children and family to carry us. That is the law today and it's not going to change anytime soon. Government will support a minimum level of care and leave the rest to our own resources.

So if you envisioned retirement as a 'flat-line' to age 90, consider a new look. You may want to adapt your pension and wealth to allow higher spending in the early "bucket-list" years, and then much later in life to support personal care and well being. (See chart in chapter 5, section 8, on missing the "flat-line".) Whether you opt to remain in or commute your pension plan, we can build strategies today that provide a designated income for health care and future spending.

As I consult with people for the life they want, we place a high value on the financial and personal freedom to tackle our 'bucket-lists' in our early retirement years, then settle into more modest spending in mid-retirement, until health eventually means spending more on personal care and comfort.

8. Can You Manage the Rising Cost of Living?

What are the terms of your pension plan? I've seen pensions without any inflation protection at all. Many offer inflation indexing of 2% to 3%. A few will match inflation up to 8%. What an astonishing difference! If we consider that long-term inflation will be at least 3% and health inflation often runs closer to 10%, we need clear answers about managing the rising cost of living.

For example: Imagine you get a pension paying $5,000/month with 3% indexing. Core inflation is 5%, with future health costs inflating near 10%. In 20 years, how much can you buy with that same $5,000? In today's purchasing power, this would represent at least a 34% drop.

Pondering this for a moment, we might say:
- 8% indexing could be a difficult plan to leave;
- 0 to 3% indexing could be hard to accept.

Consider also the onslaught of potential health costs in our later years, when the baby boomers are all clamouring for treatment, drugs or services of some sort. Wouldn't that be the time we need our greatest safeguards from inflation?

If you choose to commute and personalize your pension plan, you'll want to examine the most powerful and logical ways to match or outpace inflation over the long term. Without mentioning specific products, let me offer a glimpse of how to protect against inflation (also see section on "income mandates"):

- Dividend investments;
- Capital gains when properly diversified;
- Real estate and Infrastructure investments adding to sustainable and rising income;
- Health coverage, such as critical illness or long-term care insurance.

(NB, some people would include gold and precious metals as an inflation hedge. But anything that could potentially fall 15 years or more doesn't fit the mandate of securing retirement income. Precious metals may protect purchasing power over 50-100 year periods but they can prove vastly unreliable against inflation even in 10-20 year periods. If you want gold – and who doesn't – you may appreciate knowing gold producers can show up among broader equity and even dividend funds today.)

In summary, you want to know how a pension plan expects to increase benefits to match future costs. If the plan is adequately funded and seems secure, their current estimates of inflation indexing may survive for years into the future. If you commute your pension benefits into a personalized plan, you vitally want to know that the investments you choose will protect your purchasing power.

9. Philanthropy – Does Your Pension Play a Role?

If you've built philanthropy into your family and life values, your choice of pension can make a major impact and help you achieve results. However, this commitment to charity must be managed carefully to address potentially reduced income and costs associated with retirement.

If you're retiring and staying in the typical pension plan, you'll probably receive less than you're earning today. Over the next 10 to 20 years, your purchasing power will also be falling. If so, would you expect to continue your current level of charitable contributions? Many people on fixed-income pensions find they have to reduce their charity at a time when their hearts want to increase giving and make a higher impact for good in the community. If living costs have risen faster than pension benefits, ultimately it may be impossible to support charity as you've done in the past. If death of the pensioner will bring a sharply reduced income to the surviving spouse, he or she may have to terminate donations altogether.

This is an undesirable outcome not only for the values you hold and the charities you want to support, but also for your own financial purposes and tax planning. If there's no money left for charitable gifts, you'll also have no refund against your taxes – and no charitable receipt against taxes for your ultimate estate.

Fortunately, a personalized pension can be different in a number of ways. Let's scratch the surface on how a flexible income can be used to sustain philanthropic wishes. First, of course, you can sustain your giving if you find your income is sufficiently protected against the rising cost of living. Second, consider bequeathing to charity some or all of the remaining pension value as part of your estate planning. While residues of the traditional pension remain with the trustees, you can direct all remaining value of a commuted plan.

A third option for the personalized pension is that it can support continued planned giving through Trusts or a Charitable Community Foundation after you're gone. And finally, especially in early retirement, the flexibility of a personalized pension can support your goals of eco-tourism, foreign missions or other charitable purpose. A flexible income can help multiply the gift of your time, energy and enjoyment while sharing of yourself and your wealth along the way.

(NB: it's true that insurance strategies can increase charitable purposes regardless of which pension design you choose. I generally find however that many would feel uncomfortable initiating new costs for life insurance when moving forward into a fixed-income. I welcome if you would share your thoughts with me on this.)

Ultimately, whether you stay in a standard pension or choose a personalized pension arrangement, there are strategies that can sustain your charitable giving for life and through your estate.

10. Tax Strategies and Your Pension

Do you remember a series of "tax rage" articles that were published in the media a dozen years ago? I still find people can get angry at today's tax burdens. Even if we accept paying taxes – because it proves we had an income – we don't want to pay more than our fair share.

There are limited tax strategies from traditional pension income. Depending on where you live, you may have basic pension credits, an opportunity to split income with your spouse or certain deductions if you are developing a new business. Charitable donations can also provide tax relief.

Tax strategies may be more vigorous or generous in a personalized pension arrangement. You can explore the idea of using pension income from an older spouse to contribute and build up tax-planning strategies of a younger spouse, thus reducing your combined lifetime taxes. You can consider 'melt-down' strategies; instead of always being in a high tax rate, you'll design some years to attract less tax. Other ideas include insuring the estate to create a philanthropic gift. To maximize this strategy, you could arrange the charitable tax-relief to match the expected tax-bill on your death, with the result that your family and community can be wealthier with the way you've chosen to give.

I'm not offering tax-advice here but only sharing a larger picture of the creative discussions you can have with your professional team and tax advisors.

11. Stewarding Your Pension Decision

Your pension may be the biggest financial decision you will ever make.

In sections above, we've looked at various aspects of the contract and available options so you can decide how to protect your life income, secure the lifestyle you want to enjoy and give value to those who are dearest to you.

I believe you will also find your life aspirations and pension decisions reflected in the stories of others who have gone this route ahead of you. Was their focus life income or future estate? Were they healthy or ill? Were they retiring, re-wiring or starting a fresh new business? Whatever their circumstances and passions, you can certainly find in their stories the freedom to create your own dreams and plans.

PENSION STORIES

Pension for Marie's Grandchildren

Marie came to me, still in her 50s with an immediate wish to retire and commute the pension. I asked her why. She answered that no women in her family had ever reached 65 years of age. She felt her clock was ticking away! With a husband who also was ill, she didn't want her accumulated values staying in the pension plan. She had worked hard for years to build her pension: she didn't want their potentially early deaths to steal all this away.

It would seem silly to ask: "Who do you love more – the pension trustees and other retirees or your own family?" Marie's response was what you and I would probably answer: her children and grandchildren.

So yes, Marie instructed that her pension values be moved as a lump sum into a personalized plan. She could start drawing income immediately at a level that would support some traveling, gifting to her family and enjoying life right away. It also became the most practical support for expenses of health care for her husband and herself. When Marie and her husband have passed away, the remaining value (after any taxes) can go directly or through trusts for her children and grandchildren.

Marie's original desire was realized. She said she wanted her pension to support her own lifestyle and then benefit her family. With a personalized plan, that's exactly what's happened.

George Gets Personal Control Over his Pension

George never lost a beat since leaving the university where he was teaching. Life became simpler in some ways because he could create his own schedule, but consulting has kept this professional busier than ever. He is traveling around the world in his chosen field, using the knowledge of 30 years to help companies create and unleash value that will strengthen their own results and their countries' economies.

George is an exciting person to know. But what became clear about George's pension is that he had no interest in pulling money out of it. He simply doesn't need the income. And he didn't want the tax bill!

When George commuted his pension, the entire value flowed into a personalized account from which he can draw money at a later age. The funds will stay until George either "slows down" to unwind his consulting or reaches a point where he wants or needs to draw income. At that point, we'll finalize his desired income level to support an active lifestyle and his ongoing needs for life.

The key to George's story is that when he left the university he didn't need to replace his previous earnings. At that time, his pension income would only have caused tax headaches. So putting the value in a personalized account allowed him to delay drawing from the pension, reduce tax liabilities and then later increase the income to a level he chooses. George's personalized financial plan allowed him to address his "life horizons" on his own terms.

Pat's Pension: Seed Capital for Her Business

In 2008, Pat was leaving her employer, starting a new life in developing a business and wanting to discuss her options with me. She had significant retirement assets, but insufficient capital with which to buy or build a business. Her past experience gave her a strong foundation to follow through and establish a business that would surely thrive. All she needed was capital, and support for living expenses in the early years.

The course we charted was to commute Pat's pension so the value would be in a personal account. Next we were able to open up half the money *(the after-tax value)* quickly and use this as seed capital for the business. The other half provided an ongoing income so she could keep building her business without requiring a salary out of it.

So, how does this pan out for Pat's future? Her business has been growing. Business expenses have reduced tax on her pension income. And while pension values are reducing, her business has compensated by increasing in value. Tax planning will also bring advantages on the sale of the business to reduce or eliminate tax burdens at that time. Pat looks ahead and sees the day that selling her business will provide a rich retirement income and a healthy family estate.

In all this, Pat followed her passion to create a business. She converted taxable pension income into tax-preferred sale of a profitable business. Life income beyond that point will continue to follow tax-efficient strategies.

So this kind of situation definitely requires many competencies and capabilities in your team. Not only do we see Pat creating her dream, building a thriving business out of values from her pension. We also see that it would involve her spouse as well as her accounting, legal, and financial planning advisors.

Eric's Pension: In Sickness and In Health

Eric and his wife offer a different scenario than other stories we've considered. When Eric retired, his wife was unwell and expenses were high. Costs of ongoing treatments were accumulating on credit cards and their line of credit. You can imagine the anxiety they felt opening the mail and facing these bills.

If there's a family member with costly health concerns, this might suggest seeing your pension value as a resource for health. In Eric's case, it meant he could commute his pension to accelerate income and support his wife's health expenses. This also reduced the anxiety the couple had been facing over the debt.

An obvious concern is that Eric is spending his pension too quickly. He could be out of money by age 80 or 85. My response is simple: given his family situation, Eric made a conscientious choice to protect his remaining time with his wife. He wanted to enjoy their time together as much as possible. Once she passes, he will lower his income to a sustainable level, supplemented by her life insurance and the value of their home.

Compassion for this family is the foremost purpose for Eric being able to personalize his pension. If you're in a position like Eric and his wife, you'd have pressing needs for immediately higher income than a pension would traditionally offer. It could be due to health or other family circumstances weighing on you. Valuable help could be available through decisions related to your pension plan.

Bill's Pension: Risks and Opportunities

Bill had a tougher time deciding what to do with his pension because he and his wife had always been conservative. He expected to retire near 65 and draw the fixed-income from a pension plan. Really, why would anyone change that?

It was upon hearing a friend complain of pension cutbacks that Bill started to get concerned. The friend had worked for a well-known technology firm and always expected to live well in retirement. But after the friend retired, the pension plan suddenly cut benefits by over 30%. This hit like a bullet. And news was appearing of people in other industries whose benefits were being cut – by as much as 50%.

Bill started digging for further information. He learned that his own pension is significantly underfunded. Unless there's a miracle, his own plan will likely pay less than what the annual statements had indicated. He discovered that pension values are not the same as guaranteed deposits; there's no immediate call on government to make up any shortfall.

Making things more difficult was his advisor's guidance that if he invests in only very-low return deposits, a personalized pension plan may not support his desired income level. Staying in the fixed income of a traditional pension could be the best of difficult choices – despite possible cutbacks in his pension.

Bill faces challenging circumstances. The pension plan has much security even if underfunded; it's still going to pay some kind of income for the rest of a person's life. On the other hand, if health or estate issues arise, there may be cause to move away from the traditional pension.

We can clearly see how these matters become a personal decision. There are few, if any, no-risk options. Bill's traditional pension would suffer from the fact that it's underfunded and will likely experience an increasing numbers of people retiring and accessing the plan. Yet equally, Bill will hesitate to commute the pension because he hasn't seen or had opportunity to digest the idea of "income mandates," which will be discussed later in this book.

"Three out of four businesses will be changing leadership in the next five to ten years. "

"The majority of businesses around the world have been built by Baby Boomer entrepreneurs who, while they know how to build businesses, don't know how to transition them."

Tom Deans, <u>Every Family's Business</u>, 2008, 2009

Chapter 2

DECISIONS FOR YOUR BUSINESS

1. Lifestyles and Future Dreams while Owning a Business

How long have you been deciding to sell your business? How long have you been pondering all the things you'd have to line up to actually start taking offers? With business as a major focus of life for you and even for your family, moving toward retirement is a vitally important process. You want to enjoy the greatest success in this journey.

I often ask people: "When was your last vacation – I mean your last LONG vacation?" It's a silly question since business owners seldom leave for more than a few days, let alone weeks. So if you've been starting to consider life beyond your business, I wonder: could you get others to carry more weight and then chisel away time to go on some longer trips? Or perhaps you want an absolute clean-break by selling all at once.

The three biggest things business owners tell me they want to leave behind are:

- Grinding daily frustrations of staff and payroll issues, the flare-ups that happen in any number of ways;
- Weight of responsibility they carry for everyone else, because a wrong decision or direction in business can have major impacts on the jobs and overall wellbeing of staff, their families and customers; and
- Knowing that today's success is no guarantee for tomorrow – worries can rise and values can drop suddenly from forces in the wider economy.

While any number of factors brought you into business, there's a time you want to leave the burden of it behind – perhaps sooner rather than later.

The three biggest values business owners tell me they most want to achieve now and in their retirement include:
- Time with family and young ones "before it becomes too late;"
- Travel, including places they want to truly experience and activities they especially want to enjoy; and
- Freedom to enjoy health and life, smell a few roses, hit some balls and design a life to enjoy in all seasons.

While business owners may often feel like they are alone, there are many ways to share this journey. The following segments will show resources that have helped others move their business through a sale or succession. Stories will also zero in on specific experiences you want to capture *or avoid* along the way. You will find parallels to your own journey and, hopefully, hearing these other stories will help you formulate your plan moving forward.

2. Business Transition – Family Members, Staff or External Buyers

If you own a business and you have children working with you, you basically have two choices. One is selling outright to an external buyer or to staff members, hoping your children will be fine with the new owners. The other is a business succession to your children. This can be structured at a specific moment in time or over a prolonged period.

The main reason for delays in family succession is uncertainty about the capacity of the next generation to take leadership. Has your daughter or son really had opportunity to prove themselves as sound business owners? Maybe "yes." But you can imagine how tough it is working under a parent – especially if that parent has been totally involved in the business. Family business is a potential landmine of emotions for both children and parents. Addressing these issues may be easy or difficult – but getting them into the open is where you can get everyone working toward the needed results.

Let's say a daughter named Sally is helping with active business management; a son Ernie is mainly working 9-5 managing one of the sales regions; and a third child Becky lives several hours away teaching college fulltime. How do you manage the business interests in a way that is fair for your family? Are the three children playing equal roles? Do they carry equal responsibility in the business?

Fairness can mean many things. It does not necessarily mean treating everyone equally. It could lead to understanding what your children each need in their respective roles, and how to recognize that this business is part of their family and their own identity. It certainly means supporting (personally and financially) family members who are going to lead this business through future risks and opportunities.

In responding to these challenges, business owners can tap into resources and expertise. What results would you seek in hiring a family business facilitator? Is this a step that could be useful for your business and your family? Could this type of person help identify ways to strengthen the next generation? Could this facilitator offer added value in confirming how you see your own identity, value and contribution to life and society beyond business?

This process could lead to hiring a new permanent executive to carve certain duties away from day-to-day responsibilities of your family. On the other hand, you could consider a mentor relationship, such as a five-year CFO who is going to train family members in business leadership. Key advisors to your business can forge a pathway to the future capabilities your next generation will require.

I knew a couple who said their staff had been loyal and instrumental in the business development – so much so that this couple wanted to share ownership among the staff members. In an ideal world this might work, and it probably does sometimes. Yet staff members are most accustomed to their own lives, duties and responsibilities. They may be unable to fulfill the dreams and responsibilities of business management.

In this instance, the idea of having fifteen owners in a small business was entirely unworkable. Ultimately, I believe it was the accounting firm that pulled the plug. The business then endured a difficult reorganization. Key people left. Others remained but felt hurt and disillusioned. The couple who created this business had all these negative feelings aimed at them.

So if you face this situation, consider a good heart-to-heart with your most trusted advisors and decide what kind of consulting could be most helpful and what results you want to attain. Avoid a situation where you end up sabotaging the value you want to draw out of your business, delaying your freedom to retire. Speak early with your advisory team about the objectives you may wish to reach in sharing ownership with your team. Consider their guidance carefully to protect the vital leadership that is essential to future survival and growth. Discuss training and mentoring, cohesion of the new entity, as well as liquidity and funding, all of which will be vital preparation for this company to expand where opportunities arise.

Is your upcoming sale of the business of interest to one of the executive non-family members in your firm? If so, again I recommend working closely with your key advisors and be sure to have someone who can facilitate and mediate differing interests.   Generally, the seller wants a higher price and compensation for benefits they'll be losing in disposing of their business. Generally too, the buyer wants a lower price and to become free of any obligations to the prior owner, because it's a new day and a new person at the helm needs to drive ongoing and future values. Obviously, these issues are often resolved with time and professional support.

> ### *Footnote for advisors:*
> *A word to advisors who are reading these sections on sale and succession of business: business owners often report they haven't discussed these areas at any length. In their business, they've been battling each day's immediate issues, puzzling over how to manage family and life, and hoping you'll maintain legal and tax matters as you've done in the past.   The discussion and stories in these pages may open ways to focus on the future and allow orderly transitions in business, family, and their lives generally.*

3. Value of Professional Advisors: your "Stewardship" Team

In recent years, I've hosted an ongoing series of business seminars that feature professional advisors who can add value to your business and promote confidence in the ultimate sale of your business. A question often arises: "What does this service cost?" Of course, each professional will have his or her own answer, but the more relevant question is: "What does it cost to miss out on the value this advisor can bring?"

So in the interests of the price you want to get for your business and the freedom you want to enjoy for your future, this section will discuss the value of professional advisors serving you. You may find it particularly valuable to note the conversation you want to have with your principal advisors. That conversation will not principally be about fees, but about the value you can realize for yourself through strategies that position the eventual sale of your business.

Your business attorney, accounting firm and advisors like myself have been down this path with others. The people around you are resources to help assess the skills needed to guide your departure from the business. Your discussion with professional advisors may touch on issues of ownership, estate freeze, dividends, tax planning, and how you will structure next steps.

Business Valuation is a critical service for any business considering a sale. It may be among the services your accounting firm provides; others will bring in an independent and certified business valuator or you can identify one yourself.   Becoming a certified business valuator is an intense and prolonged process and that's why these people come with a couple of designations, typically CA or CPA and a CBV.

Two fundamental approaches to valuation will start either with earnings or with assets, depending on the nature and specifics of your business. Asset valuation is easier and more straightforward than an earnings valuation. You can get an appraisal on values of land, buildings, equipment, inventory, and goodwill if such will be relevant to a buyer. Whatever can be given a market price based on asset value would go into this equation: after negotiating any adjustments you would approach the reasonable valuation of the business assets.

Earnings will reflect "true earnings" after being normalized for various kinds of adjustments. These can include many factors. Were you keeping money in the business and paying yourself less than a buyer would do or were you treating the business as a cash cow and piggy bank, drawing cash out of the business? Earnings would adjust in expectation accordingly. Then the valuator will provide reason for a specific "multiple," such as 2 x earnings or 4 x earnings, to reach an estimated "enterprise value." Subtracting debts that continue with the business leaves the amount you hope to receive in selling your business, or its deemed fair market value.

A Business Broker can manage the process of selling your business. Marketing your business isn't putting a "for sale" sign on it. In fact, you wouldn't do that. Privacy is essential because you don't want current suppliers or clients moving away from you on the assumption that you're leaving the business. In the worst scenario, if a business is "for sale" and yet doesn't sell over a prolonged period that can severely damage confidence of all parties – with obvious jeopardy to any final selling price.

An experienced business intermediary or business broker will promote your business quietly and safely among a variety of groups as desired. These can include: (i) financial buyers, (ii) strategic buyers, (iii) corporate suitors, and (iv) private equity groups. Your conversations with the broker and your key advisors will focus on the right positioning to achieve success.

It's often asked, how quickly can things sell? Surveys suggest at least nine months to a year or more. More to the point, the value of a strong team is proven in its capacity to sell a business at all, for reasonable price, rather than stalling for years. Persistence, prudence and a strong team can get your deal done.

Legal Guidance. Legal guidance is vital, and it's best to realize this early so you can avoid possible disappointments, delays and unwanted liabilities – or the derailing of your deal.

Business law is a distinct specialty. I cannot stress strongly enough that other branches of law, such as real estate, are no preparation for the attention and experience you want from a business attorney. Here are some things to bear in mind.

First, be sure you have legal affairs in order, with an up-to-date Minute Book, suitable contracts with all major suppliers and clear employment and confidentiality agreements with your employees. Get everything clear and orderly in preparation for suitors' "due diligence review." Your attorney's work will help secure the value in selling your business and will seek to move future liabilities and responsibilities to the buyer and away from yourself. In non-disclosure agreements, letters of intent, and anything else in this process, you'll find that the insight, coaching, expertise and confidence you gain with an experienced business attorney is not a cost but a value.

You might have assumed there's no need for an estate lawyer when preparing to transition your business. However, estate planning can be deeply connected to changes coming in your business. Much like a business attorney, an estate lawyer has expertise and knowledge in all aspects of estate planning, including wills, power of attorney, trusts, amongst others.

Certified Financial Planner. All of these professional services come within the wider discussion of financial planning. Many people don't realize the degree to which insurance- and financial planning are largely unregulated. In many jurisdictions one can hang a shingle and call themselves a financial planner without any of the clear education, experience and regulatory oversight you would expect.

A Google search for "how to find a financial planner" yields half-a-billion results. Searching "find a certified financial planner" yields over two million results. Adding your community's name in the search seems to show national firms with captive employees.

How therefore will you know if someone is an accredited, trustworthy and long-term financial planner? One way is to meet them and consider if this is a person bringing real value to your situation. Another is to learn how others have experienced working with this planner. Third is to check their designations and whether these represent the level of experience you require. Other professionals in your community can also confirm, and you may get their endorsement for a planner you'd choose to serve you.

> **Footnote**: You may have noticed a veritable alphabet-soup of designations after advisors' names. Some designations are more localized while others have international recognition. An Internet search will show what these letters mean and how the advisor may be prepared to serve you.

4. Turning your Business into a Life Income

What are the financial strategies that support life income – particularly when it comes to avoiding key errors that have cost people much of their wealth? I too often see people struggling to live in poor circumstances when they could have been safe, financially secure and enjoying life.

For the moment, I want you to get a mental image of your current investments. Would you say that you've generally invested like other people do? Or are your investments distinct because of the business you own? The reason for this question is that most readers may own a small-to-mid-sized business and yet you'd likely say your investments are similar to others. You might never have wondered about this, but if your business is "equity" even being small or mid-cap, wouldn't it make sense to take a more conservative position in your other invested assets?

Then again when you sell your business and retire, you will be selling off a significant piece of equity, right? So how will you capture and express this in your investing, when you've suddenly sold off the biggest equity you've ever owned. You should consider what kinds of equity would best contribute to protect your income and allow for cost-of-living increases through the years ahead.

I share this with you because I've found much planning to be silent on this, omitting the relationship between one's business and transitions with the investment portfolio. I will later suggest a five-finger (or five-mandate) approach that can enhance security while owning a business, and also vigorously contribute to a sustainable income when the business is sold and the assets are needed to support the rest of your life. We'll touch on a combination of dividends, infrastructure, real estate, global fixed-income and later use of life payout annuities.

5. Estate Planning Issues for You and Your Family

How have you considered the estate planning side of your business? Do you realize you may never spend all your money? Wealth breeds more wealth, and yet wealth doesn't always sit well within families. You know that instinctively, and you've heard stories that support this.

Many business owners have already established estate plans, and some of this planning will need to be clarified or re-built due to sale or transition of the business. For instance, you might have had a separate will for your business *(in some jurisdictions you can do this),* but after selling your business you would need your primary will and estate planning to address wealth issues upon death, such as inheritance, charitable giving and trusts. Or your will may have stated the requirement of including your business attorney, whereas this would no longer be necessary once you've sold or separated yourself from the business. As well, your current will might authorize your executor to have or share authority over your business in event of death, but after disposing the business you will likely have different wishes for care and distribution of your total invested wealth.

Upon selling the business, you should confirm or clarify purposes of your wills, powers of attorney, personal or family trusts, and so on. If you have family or even if you don't, ask the question: What planning would bring the most peace of mind and express powerfully and fittingly the value that your life represents and how you want to be remembered?

6. Loss of Heath/Dental and Other Insurance

Everyone asks about this, even though you may think it a minor issue compared to the business. Let's take a quick look.

If you're selling the business, your group health and dental benefits may terminate. However, you have some options available if you act promptly. You can arrange to convert and continue your old benefits fairly seamlessly but there is a strict time period – usually 60 days – in which you must apply for this option. Another choice if you're very healthy is to consider delaying the expense of benefits and picking up the coverage at a later time. Or your spouse may have continuing coverage at work or via a retiree plan, so you might waive private coverage for now. You can also choose a retail plan for the health coverage you choose, based on your insurability and the use of any medications and treatments you are already using.

If your family is continuing with the business or you are continuing in some reduced capacity, it's possible you may continue on the company's health and dental plan. Be aware that expenses you put on the plan will increase costs of future renewals. This situation could cause a smaller business to eventually cancel coverage, thus threatening the health coverage that younger staff need and expect as part of their employment.

Another point to consider is changing the disability coverage you've had under your business into private critical-illness or long-term care insurance. This can provide resources when health fails or ongoing personal care treatments are required.

Have you pondered the value of key-person life insurances that you can re-deploy for spousal support, pension maximization, or estate planning? Sale or transition of a business might seem like a time to cancel insurances, but reflecting on some of these items above could be worth a fortune for your own health and your estate planning.

7. Stewarding your Business Decisions

How you want to transition your business for succession – and what you want out of this process – are among the largest financial decisions you will ever make.

We've looked at matters of succession within a family, transition to staff, and sale to outside interests. We've also considered the professionals who can support you in valuation, marketing, accounting, business law, estate law and financial planning. We know you have bigger dreams to enjoy, and a freedom you want to explore outside of your business while you have strength and energy.

In the coming pages, you will find some elements of your story and aspirations in the experiences of others who have gone this route ahead of you. As you ponder these, make some notes on your personal feelings. Consider getting the "price-tag" you want from your business, securing a life income for your journey and estate planning to fulfill your desired gifts for family and/or philanthropy. These stories will introduce some interesting twists. Hopefully, they will open some opportunities and sharpen your thoughts about your future.

BUSINESS STORIES

Linda's Story: Too Conservative?

Linda completed the sale of her business when she was 62 years old. The sale value of her business resulted in a significant amount of money that would allow her to live comfortably for a fairly long time. Yet it wasn't enough that she could spend without limits or that she wouldn't run out of capital while still living. So a key for Linda's security was to ensure we "layered" income strategies that would continue to protect her for life.

The other main factor for Linda was that she felt hesitant about financial risk. She wasn't one to invest in the stock market because she didn't want any losses. Her worry meant she'd only invest in financial products paying near the rate of inflation or even less. That is risky! For example, if guaranteed deposits were paying 3% and inflation is going to eat that up and more, then Linda should realize she will run out of money someday. That is the biggest thing Linda wants to avoid, right?

We needed a program to guarantee a continuing life income for Linda that can also increase over time. It also had to give some flexibility in case Linda's needs change or a sudden event occurs from health or other circumstance that she'd need some money quickly.

Speaking very broadly, the approach we took was a "five-mandate process" for income planning. This includes income streams from dividends, real estate, infrastructure, and a combination of guaranteed and strategic fixed-income. There could also be cash-values from life insurance policies, or the income from long-term care insurance when age brings higher costs for personal care.

Keep in mind that Linda's greatest risk was running out of money before she runs out of time. Her wealth could be spent before she turned 75. Would she then turn to family for support, at the very point they're making final preparations for their own retirement! Surely Linda wants to avoid being a burden to her family in this way, so she needs to learn – with the right professional support – how she can attract inflation-protected income that can protect her to age 90 or beyond.

Beth's Story: Seeding a New Family Enterprise

I bring you Beth's story because not everyone will just sell a business and move on to greener pastures. A great opportunity gave Beth good value for her business. Now, she can live life larger and travel more widely and freely than she ever could do when she owned the business. But as we also see here, Beth will help start another business in her family.

Beth came out with $3Million after-tax from the sale of her business and all has cleared. She's taking an interest in a business one of her children is building. In her mind, she has set aside up to $1Million for the child's business, together with her time and consultation to accelerate opportunities in that business.

$2Million then remains to support Beth's lifestyle and dreams through the years ahead. As for the $1Million investment, it's not guaranteed what will happen with that; it could grow, it could flop. So Beth's security and her ultimate estate dreams for two other children and the family as a whole must be served by the $2Million Beth is ready to invest. She will be very interested to avoid the financial hazards and mistakes we are addressing later in this book.

Beth's story shows that sale of a business may lead to partial retirement combined with new business interests. We must be sure and protect Beth's well being whether or not her new business succeeds. We need reliable financial strategies to assure Beth's income for life.

Toms' Story – Is it the Money or the Time?

Tom was 73 and tiring of the business he had built over fifteen years. The hours and attention he had to pay to staffing, the anxiety about so many factors in his business was wearing him down. His wife felt the same way and she saw the toll this was taking on Tom. She knew the dreams they were missing out on as selling the business went on to another year, and another year.

I asked Tom how much he wanted for his business. He quickly replied, "$2.2Million." It sounded fair, and I asked him how he had come up with this number. He recited the math he had calculated again and again for himself and told me that if he sold for anything less, he wouldn't have enough money. I also asked, what would the market pay you today for this business? He looked down to the table quietly and replied that his best offer had been $1.7Million.

So we worked through the numbers to find potential solutions. Selling for $2.2Million could give Tom about $1.3Million after covering debt, fees and taxes. Tom was firm then about his asking price because he didn't want to live on anything less than $1.3Million. If he accepted $1.7Million as a sale, his life would never achieve what he wanted.

This now moved us into the personal values around life and family, and what he would enjoy most once the business would be sold. We looked at the income he needed, and some estate value he wanted to preserve, certainly for his wife and also for their children and grandchildren.

When I came back to Tom the next time I had a surprise for him, and this changed the conversation. Tom had figured he could safely expect 3-4% earnings on an investment, and then pay full-tax on those earnings and end up with less than $40,000 annual income. Combined with other pension and savings, this wouldn't let them live the way they wanted, so Tom was committed to getting $2.2Million.

Things looked very different when we were able to combine income-strategies for 6% at a lower tax rate! In the financial structure we put together, we found Tom and his wife could accomplish what they wanted even at $1.7 Million. The truth was that he hadn't known how to optimize his income for lower-tax and lifetime security.

Sure enough Tom still had the habit of wanting $2.2Million for the business. Our conversation now turned from "price" to "life." "So Tom", I explained, "it's clear you can get enough money today to safely sell your business and enjoy life on your own terms." He agreed. I added, "and given time you may even reach the desired price you've had in mind, even the $2.2M." He listened intently. "So I want to ask you Tom, if you wait say another two or three years and get the full price you've been seeking, can you buy back the time?" "No", he said, "I can't buy back the time."

On that thought he scratched the back of his hand, deep in thought. I felt he was pondering the ongoing stresses and dreams postponed. Golf courses and friendships were beckoning him, near and far, and the focus now turned more fully toward the life he and his wife could enjoy.

The oddest thing happened: Tom woke up the next morning still hesitating about selling the business or to seek a better deal that he couldn't yet achieve. On reflection, we realize that Tom enjoys the socialization and friendships of people through his work. There are many reasons a person may stay in business beyond financial need. But the point is: Tom can choose to sell and retire anytime he wishes, as long as the market doesn't fall away for his business. For now, Tom can safely sell and walk into the lifestyle he chooses, as soon as he's ready.

Gino and Frank's Story: The Missing $3 Million

Gino and Frank had a company that would never sell. That's what the accountant told me. On its course at that time, the business seemed destined to fail and terminate the jobs of three dozen employees. Gino and Frank were firm that they wouldn't sell to anyone for less than $8Million. The accountant said this business wouldn't attract any more than $5Million. Given their ages (near 70), the missing $3 million was an impasse that could not be bridged.

I brought a NEW question. I asked if these gentlemen would actually spend $8Million after selling the business. The accountant said that was unlikely, as they'd never spent like that in their whole lives. On this basis, I offered a possibility that we might be able to find the missing $3Million! Further meetings ensued with the sellers and buyer, and we came to find ourselves on the right course.

Here's the high level picture. Gino and Frank weren't going to spend millions, but they did want the pride of sale, the pat-on-the-back in getting their price. They also wanted compensation for losing the opportunity of tapping their business as a private piggy bank, paying some of their personal expenses that after-sale would be paid from their own bank accounts. A solution could only arise if we could identify a new structure of financial rewards to secure what they needed.

Working together as a team – with their accounting firm – we finalized an approach to pay Frank and Gino a few million up front plus a consulting income for the first two years, plus dividends. The remaining amount wasn't money they'd spend in this lifetime so we found a different currency in which to pay them. Call it a "later" currency, or actually just call it life insurance that would finalize the buy-out from their estates. The cost was less than 5% deposit per year (*even less than paying interest if the money had been borrowed*) and the debt was secured by preferred shares. The new owners successfully built the firm with new energy, protecting employees and wider community interests as the business continued strongly.

Pause and consider – isn't money always inevitably about life? So what did Gino and Frank get from this? They shed day-to-day responsibilities and got the freedom to relax and enjoy more time with other family and life experiences. They got high value, including lower-tax dividends and payment to their estate.

Don and Elizabeth's Story: An Estate Issue

Don and Elizabeth already completed the sale of their business and put their final legal affairs in order some years ago. Or so they thought.

Their business lawyer had done the wills, and this had left their estate in a precarious state in the event of death. Now in their mid-70s they were referred to me in respect of income and investments, yet the estate planning soon appeared as an equally vital issue.

In their case, an only child was appointed to be executor. Yet what the original lawyer failed to realize was that the child has been chronically disabled and also financially compromised. Even if this adult-child could serve as executor, the parents said the estate would be spent and gone within a year or two.

With an estate lawyer we clarified the values Elizabeth and Don most wanted to express in their estate, including an income for their only child, and ultimate value through trusts for their grandchildren. Their message of love, harmony and responsibility are vital as they complete their estate planning and ultimate gifts.

"Selling a business is one of the most important decisions in a business owner's life. It is filled with excitement and numerous other emotions, including fear, anxiety, and uncertainty about the future. ... There are only two ways for owners to get out of the trench. One is to be pro-active .... The other is to be reactive....."

Doug Robbins, <u>There's Always a way to Sell Your Business</u>, 2010

Chapter 3

INHERITING WEALTH

You probably know that a younger generation will inherit quite a bit of money from their parents or grandparents in the next few decades. It often comes with wonderful heartstrings attached. Whether it's $50,000 or $5Million being received, I want to advocate for a sense of the "values" that may come with this money. These personal values and wishes can be a vital part of the legacy you're receiving.

Usually, an inheritance is accompanied with strong feelings. These can run the full gamut from joy and gratitude on the one hand, to guilt or disgust on the other. Families come in all stripes and colours and none of us are able to choose the family into which we're born. However, we can choose to honour the highest values of any money that arrives by inheritance.

Much has been written elsewhere on the experiences of inheriting money. I'm not focusing on that discussion at this time. See the later chapter on how you can be prepared to avoid the most costly and aggravating financial mistakes others have made. We can learn much through the experiences of other people. Hearing their stories can crystallize our perspective and help us make wise decisions to protect what we want for the future.

An associate of mine tells the story of what happened after his father died. His mother was receiving requests – mostly fraudulent – for money that she had access to, and she believed she was investing the money wisely. After a time, she admitted the problem to her family. They asked: "How much did you lose, mom?" And reflecting on the years that she and her husband had worked so hard together she answered: "About five years – everything that we earned over the final five years of our business." This could have been avoided with open communication, trust and respect for values.

With my own clients, I make a point of knowing and recording their "values" around money and what they would communicate to the generation receiving the inheritance. This combines the legacies of hand and heart, earth and spirit, wealth and core values. It expresses what wealth has meant to the senior generation and what it may mean to the heirs who are willing to listen and reflect on this.

For example, a wife and husband among my clients were born in Europe and shared with me many powerful memories of their childhood in the Great Depression and Second World War. They moved to Canada in the 1950s and worked hard for more than forty more years, providing tremendous opportunity for their children and grandchildren. When there is an estate to be settled and insurance money to be paid out, I will be with the family and help share the values this couple shared with me, and how the inheritance conveys a gift of love, life, and rich meaning to their loved ones.

Another household had been constantly struggling over money. The debt load they were trying to carry was a perpetual worry, and seemingly getting deeper. Then an inheritance arrived. As with many couples, one was more of a spender while the other was more of a saver. You might guess how they saw the opportunity represented in this inheritance. Was this money an opportunity to break away and relax, get a "real vacation" and buy a new car? Or was this money an opportunity to eliminate high-cost debt and reduce their mortgage to a level they could more easily manage? Discussing the opportunities openly can help avoid resentment and allow people to see that reducing debt will ease their tensions – and with monthly savings allow them to upgrade the car or plan a trip in the coming year or so. Allowing time to create the best results with this money can truly change their lives for the better.

Another family carried a message of avoiding the stock market, preferring the security of real estate and life insurance. This seemed a bit awkward because the heir had a broader outlook on investing, feeling capable of managing stock market equities. Personal reflection, however, suggested an opportunity to honour the parents' feelings, even though they were deceased. The solution was a sequence of profitable investments in real estate and life insurance that would strengthen the heir and family, while conveying the full value of the inheritance onto the 3rd generation. Looking back now years later, there has never been a "meltdown" in this investment decision, and it has continued very profitably.

A family law consideration would arise in discussing your inheritance with the right lawyer, or possibly also with a well experienced financial advisor. Ask what kinds of considerations would protect your inheritance in the event of your divorce or re-marriage. In your jurisdiction/place of residence, will an inheritance be held sacred as something you own apart from your spouse? Would mingling the value of that inheritance by purchasing a home or paying down a mortgage cause this value to be deemed "family property" and thus available for a split of assets in the event of divorce? What distinctions would further allow any life insurance benefits to avoid such family law divisions? Be aware of any guidelines in the will that ask you to protect the inheritance, so it remains within the direct line of your family rather than walking out the door someday with an ex-spouse. This discussion ranks with pre-nuptials in the pillow-talk people feel awkward having, yet the result is clarity, safety and truly honouring the values of those who have given so much of themselves to you.

"Cascading wealth" is worth mentioning here. My grandparents gave something to my parents. My parents gave something to me. I plan and prepare estate value that my children will receive – and so on to their children as far as the future will go. The question is one of balance in financial and insurance planning. Can you inherit a sum of money, which creates an income and growth that will reward you wonderfully while you are living, and yet fully and safely move also to the next generation? The answer is "yes." Wealthy people have accomplished this for many generations, and we're continuing this still today. Wills, trusts, investments and insurance can support this cascading wealth.

We've only touched the surface here. Thousands of well-written articles will offer further ideas. There are two fundamental values I am offering that perhaps you wouldn't find most other places. The first is to recognize and honour the values of those who have bequeathed their wealth to you. This can offer tremendous guidance in how you apply this wealth for your own wellbeing now and for the future. The second is to not risk that money because it may never come again: this might be your only shot at sudden wealth.

Protect the value you inherit. Enjoy it carefully in your own lifetime. Consider how to convey similar value on to your children or other heirs who follow. "Cascading wealth" is a vision, a magic, a love that can keep the gift growing and giving from generation to generation.

Chapter 4

WINNINGS AND WINDFALLS

They say the easiest way to a small fortune is to begin with a large fortune. I want to share with you how you can protect your wealth, and also enjoy what you want it to mean for your life and loved ones.

Let's consider the unique experience of windfalls and sudden wealth events and the specific impact they can have on you. We want to ensure that moving forward, you will enjoy the confidence and happiness of doing the right things with your money.

Decades of research prove what major religions have always known: that money alone doesn't bring happiness. A sudden influx of it can bring an immediate thrill, but that wears off too easily as life pales in comparison to the day you won the "big one." As a result, life may seem more mundane and uneventful after winning, leaving people less rather than more happy.

I've worked with people in professional capacities for over three decades. What amazed me long ago was that when people told me the stories of their lives, they tended to forget the events that had spurred the greatest immediate thrill. I learned that people experience the greatest value in life through its hurdles and hard-won successes. If a "big win" puts you on "easy street" and all your troubles are gone, you may find yourself questioning life and searching how to get happy again. That's a trigger for losing it all – as a vast majority of lottery winners have done.

Sudden wealth can introduce anxiety into family and friendships. Lesser-known relatives may appear. Old "friends" arrive with hands outstretched. Innocently helping someone can evoke the feeling that it was nothing for you, or somehow you owed it to them. All too easily, winnings can bring loneliness and disruption of existing relationships. Media stories also mention kidnappings, murder, and having to leave one's community for a new start elsewhere. Luckier it may be to fantasize about winning rather than actually winning. My focus is really about ensuring how you can be safe and enjoy life without the downside risks that have hurt others.

Winning a fortune means it's time – immediately – to ensure you have the right professional advisors serving you. Would you manage this much wealth without a certified advisor and a financial plan that guides how the money will be invested and safely secured? Would you not want professional accounting to help confirm strategies and reduce tax? Would you not want an estate lawyer to help you instruct who among family or charity should receive this money when you die? Or how decisions would be made for your personal care, and who would make such decisions, if you were ill or incapacitated? Should you consider counsel to help you discuss this wealth with family members, and thus aim to strengthen relationships and protect opportunities for those dearest to you? In many places you'll also want an expert insurance advisor who, in alliance with the estate lawyer, can help shelter winnings from estate taxes. The kinds of people I mention here can help comprise your "stewardship team" to guide what your windfall can mean for you.

A client of mine won a lottery some years ago. He pondered this with close members of his family: they had emigrated from another country and all had worked extremely hard to achieve their success here. His decision as a winner was that he would continue life with as little change as possible. Though a young man, he didn't want to impress his soon-to-be bride. He also didn't want to show off to neighbours or anyone else. He quietly paid mortgages for his parents and siblings, and bought a home for himself, which continues to be their home even now. He has continued in the same work. Being free of a mortgage has meant the financial capacity to travel a bit more than other people, and create experiences that will always be memorable for his young family. This is an entirely untarnished story of winning!

Others may want to live large and spend. This is natural, and the wisest approach to this is taking a specific sum or percentage of the money and "blow it" having an awesome time in a way that contributes to your happiness and future memories. For example, if you blow 10% of this jackpot making memories and put 90% of it into a structured and strategic financial plan, you can enjoy financial security and unbounded opportunities for life!

Make debt a thing of the past. I didn't mention this above because I know the desire to spend something first and face the debt later. So now, after you've blown 5% or 10% of your winning, pay off all your debt. No other investment is going to give you as much freedom as being debt free at this time of your life.

Consider "giving." Many have realized it's more rewarding giving $20 to someone in need, than finding $20 on the sidewalk. Ponder this yourself. Will you donate a portion of your winning to charity? Would you be happy having the ability to do this? Will you engage a certified advisor to create a financial plan through which you can continue giving forever? I'd probably ignore the people who come knocking on the door or ringing your phone. Find an advisor in philanthropy or a leader in your community foundation *(typically an umbrella for support toward any or all charities)* to help you identify first your personal values and motivations as a giver, and second how to initiate and engage as a philanthropist locally and even globally.

If there is a magical sequence to living successfully with sudden wealth and winnings I would say it is this: secure a life-long income from your winnings, and then make gradual adaptations to lifestyle. Once you've paid off all debts, bought a holiday and made a discrete gift to charity, put the rest safely into a short-term investment giving you time to sit down with the right advisors and build a long term plan for this money. When you're doing this, a combination of investments can: (i) supplement your monthly income for life, (ii) allow occasional withdrawals for special purposes, (iii) provide a planned approach that can help family members, (iv) establish a platform for philanthropy, (v) consider possible career change through further study or business development.

Now you can also turn a page into the next chapter on avoiding key mistakes that threaten peoples' wealth and steal their money away. You can avoid being separated from your wealth. Perhaps it came to you quickly – as easily as picking random numbers against infinite odds. But I promise, you can beat the odds of losing all this!

Chapter 5

MISTAKES TO AVOID IN FINANCIAL PLANNING

I know a woman who many years ago didn't realize her car needed regular check-ups or oil changes. She filled it with gasoline, topped up the wiper fluid, but gave it no further thought when turning on the ignition. One day her car didn't start. While fretting about the bill, she wondered how serious the estimate would be. She learned something new and valuable that day – that you cannot drive a car 80,000 kilometers without an oil change. Eventually, everything in life needs some attention.

The same is true for our financial well being. Proper care and stewardship can help you avoid nightmare problems, allowing you to truly protect and perpetuate your wealth for the goals you want to enjoy. So let's dig in. Here are some mistakes or omissions that I find to be all too common. Avoiding such mistakes can be a rich advantage for your life, wealth and future estate.

1. No Lifestyle Plan – Fixating on Money Instead of Life

A frequent mistake is focusing on money more than life. It's especially common in sudden-wealth situations, and crushingly so in the case of lump-sum sale proceeds, a sizeable inheritance or winnings that all too soon disappear. There are many ways people can focus too much on the money and miss the true value that money can represent in their lives.

In the earlier story of Tom, we found him postponing the sale of his business to get a price much higher than the market would offer. When I agreed he could wait a couple of years and probably get his price, he then agreed that he wouldn't be able to buy back the time. His wife couldn't buy back the time either, nor the friends he'd rather be golfing with in Florida or Scotland. When all was said and done, Tom wanted to be free of the business NOW and enjoy his life freely. So our attention turned to financial strategies that would assure Tom's income from the current value of his business. Now, he could move his life forward without delay.

Pension and other financial decisions can also focus our minds too much on the money, and less on the life we are trying to achieve. A pension could mean a fixed allowance for the rest of your life, or a lump sum with which you can make more flexible lifestyle choices. An inheritance could mean spending it away, or designing how to increase resources and happiness for the rest of your life. Winning a lottery could mean luxury vacations and new cars for a few years, or creating the base of lifelong financial security for yourself and future generations.

If we first determine what we want our life to be about, then we can align what money should do to fit our chosen lifestyle. Some key questions to consider include: What are the most important experiences I want to enjoy right away? Where do I want to be in three years, five years or twenty years? How do I want to impact other peoples' lives, especially family and community? If I were looking back on this moment from my deathbed, what result would I want to achieve? How would I like to be remembered?

I sometimes share a sketch that caught my eye in a magazine a few years ago. This fellow had just retired and his wife was presenting him with a wonderful gift and a large cake to celebrate. You could see that the gift wasn't at all what the fellow wanted. He had not communicated, or perhaps his wife had misunderstood what he said. And this is the thing: poor communication can lead to disagreements about money, retirement and lifestyle.

So if an influx of money – whether lump sum or monthly income – is about to suddenly come into your life, have you spent time with the most important people in your life to discuss goals, needs and expectations? Who was the wife that told her husband, "I married you for better or for worse but not for lunch!" because she already has a fully developed pattern of how she was spending her time? One partner wants to drive North America in an RV for half the year while the other would keep their social calendar at home while flying away for short trips to beaches and mountains. Consider that your new life – even retirement – takes practice. Why not explore and discuss together how you'll build the activities and interests that you will enjoy most?

2. A Problem of Eggs: Too Few or the Fear of Too Few

Some people assumed they had enough eggs in their basket to retire and bask in the sun. Winning a few million dollars could keep you for five or ten years, but it disappears like water through your fingers. The same applies with an inheritance: it can make a major impact for good or a few wrong choices can steal it forever.

A couple with stretched savings was sitting in their advisor's office when he said: "So what kind of work do you want to do now that you're retired?" Obviously that wasn't their desire, and being forced back to the treadmill isn't anyone's dream for the future.

If you're selling a business or have come up with a sizable pot of money with which to plan your future, make sure you're going to be safe. Review the expenses you would incur in retirement – what your desired lifestyle will cost. Look at inflation, health costs, even things you might formerly have paid for through your business. Combine all your resources that include your savings, sale of business, pension values, household equity, value you can draw from insurance and other tax-sheltered plans, and determine right now if you have enough eggs in your basket to safely support your life to at least age 90. Why not test it through to 105 just for extra comfort.

The opposite notion is that you don't have enough eggs in your basket. It can be a paralyzing fear that you'll run out of money and hence never feel safe enough to retire. One of my clients was 69 and a leading professional in his field when I started to realize the conflict between my planning and his lack of decision. He would often visit or call me. I'm no doctor, but I could tell his blood pressure was rising and his face was looking flushed and unhealthy. We spoke about his work, a schedule that kept him traveling five days a week. He admitted to me that his doctor wanted him to retire: he was at risk of dying before he would ever retire. On the decision to retire, he was paralyzed with the fear of "too few eggs."

So every few months we'd speak and I would assure him: "we've worked these numbers over and over in recent years and we know you can retire the moment you choose to do so." While it was a troubling decision, I'm happy to share that he retired successfully at 73. Each review since then proves that his assets are still growing and life is good. He now grasps that there are enough eggs to protect his income for life and also provide a healthy estate for his family. In terms of lifestyle, he's active, happy, smiles more, enjoys more time with his family, shares in the cooking and continues to enjoy carpentry and other hobbies. In short, he is thrilled that he got past that paralyzing fear of retiring so he could move forward to enjoy the life he has now.

3. Future Costs: Inflation and Health Care

Wherever money comes from, it disappears quickly enough through inflation. Call this a "silent thief" or a "hidden tax." By any name, inflation will eat and steal away your purchasing power. You need a vigorous plan to overcome this. Ignore it at your peril. You may feel inflation is tame near 3%. But in ten years time, 3% inflation means a 25% cut in purchasing power. In 20 years, it's close to a 50% cut in purchasing power. Would you accept a contract today guaranteeing to pay you 25% less in ten years, 50% less in 20 years, and to keep falling as long as you live? Unless you put a leash on inflation, this is what happens.

Imagine winning or inheriting wealth at a younger age. Perhaps you spend a good chunk of it and hopefully pay off your debts, and then feel the rest will keep you for life. But after 30 years inflation has eaten away 60% of the value. 40 years without proper planning can destroy 75% of this nest egg.

Inflation can utterly destroy the value of money. Given enough time, purchasing power will approach zero. The strategies we bring together for your financial planning are therefore essential to preserve and create value that will outpace the losses due to inflation.

Worse than core inflation is health inflation. At any age, you could suffer illness and require ongoing need for personal care; the goliath inflation we need to beat is health care. While we all know health costs are rising, very few have addressed this in their personal and financial planning.

To put this in perspective, we know that health costs rise ten-fold from age 65 to 85. We also know that a bulging baby boom generation is moving into the 65+ age bracket. The impact on our personal finances and on government and business will be astronomical. In 2009, the International Monetary Fund described future health costs of the baby-boom generation as ten-times greater than the 2008 worldwide financial meltdown. No government, no pension plan, no investment plan, and no family will be free of the impact of these events – unless you have a vigorous financial plan with the resources to match this inflationary beast.

Health costs aren't just a head-on collision; they're a locomotive barreling down the tracks toward our generation. The lights are pointed where we'll be standing. Our government leaders are fully aware of this. They're totally occupied with today's leading issues and desperately unarmed against such health costs of the future. We can conclude with certainty, as costs rise, government response will fall. Those who are unprepared will fall and become the legal burden of their children or grandchildren. And when the latter are ready to retire, they'll be carrying their parents' medical expenses instead.

So look at the assets you own today. Think ahead also to what you expect to own ten years from now, or further into the future. Consider your house, pension values, cottage or other real estate, savings and investment plans, insurance for life and health, education plans for children or grandchildren, boats, cars, musical instruments, works of art, and so on. Review each of these in your mind for a moment and answer the question – which of these would you most willingly use to pay for personal care when illness and decreased capacities come into your life? Which asset would you be willing to lose – or frankly which would you dedicate today – for the purpose of paying future health costs? What taxes would hit when you do so? What would be your loss of enjoyment in such property? Who else would lose – spouse, family – when you are forced to spend that asset?

For me, the asset I'm most willing to spend is my health insurance. Part of it will pay a sizable lump sum if a critical event occurs. Another part will pay an ongoing income to match health costs. This protects the rest of my assets, and prevents me from triggering taxes on the disposal of assets.

Certified financial planning can fully address the impact of inflation in general and health inflation in particular. When you open your financial plan – whether as a hard copy in your home or an e-file on your computer – does it address the issues of inflation and future health costs? Start a process immediately to layer a combination of your financial resources and insurance that can guard your comfort in the years ahead.

Many sources confirm that health costs generally rise 10-fold (1000%) from age 65 to 80. Plus the following:

"According to the IMF, the toll of aging on G20 nations will be 10 times that of the (2008) financial crisis."

"Today's ...realistic and dismal demographic scenario is that the number of older people will grow faster than younger ones almost everywhere in the world."

Edward Yardeni, in The Globe And Mail, July 9th, 2009.

4. Lack of Guidance and DIY

They say that 70% of lawyers don't have wills, and 70% of people with $5Million to invest are still lacking a financial plan. Apparently, this has remained unchanged for years. I wonder what people are waiting for – what would trigger a change to have their estate and financial planning in proper order?

There has been a certain level of dismay with the financial industry because anyone can call themselves a planner, even if they were really just selling investments. Long ago, I took my car to someone who wasn't really a mechanic; the results were, of course, sub-standard.

Today, we take our cars to accredited mechanics. We also trust medical specialists for our health care. Now too, when it comes to your total wealth, financial security and personal goals, wouldn't you choose someone who is certified to advise and align the results you want to achieve? We have a veritable alphabet soup of designations in the world today: looking them up online will show if they're an in-house certificate at some firm, or specific to a region or country, or internationally recognized as a standard of financial practice and ethics.

I've known advisors whose common-sense and "do-no-harm" attitude offered good care even without designations. "Letters" don't guarantee integrity or excellence. So knowing your advisor, or receiving a strong referral from another professional, can support the confidence you have, regardless of what letters an advisor may or may not have after their name.

Do-It-Yourself is another approach. I've never done this with my health or my car, but I know some people over the years have given up on investment advisors. DIY may work for some people; when it doesn't those people tend to stay silent. Software is easily available on the Internet to help people with a DIY approach; if it doesn't work, it quietly disappears. Since such failures, like shame, turn to silence we tend not to hear when DIY brings disaster.

I can't personally verify all of the following information but I've heard that the 1990s offered raw stock market returns near 17% per year in the U.S.A. DIY investors however earned less than 4% per year. We can surmise the cause, but the results speak loudest. DIY was extremely costly to many investors. A further study was built on the question of how many DIY investors could keep pace with the natural and raw returns of the market. I recall the study took place in Taiwan, and the answer as I remember was 0.6% of investors who could over time show some capacity to keep up with or exceed the market. Nearly 99% of people then who choose to invest on their own are at jeopardy of losing a modest or vast sum compared to natural raw numbers of the market.

You may have distinct knowledge of your industry that sets you apart from others – it gives you an edge you can perhaps legally use in your DIY investment choices. I realize this is so. I've also learned from clients who were in such position that this unique advantage can disappear within three to six months of retiring. Thus, they value even more strongly the importance of professional financial planning.

This also fits the bigger picture of how your professional advisors can work together as a "stewardship team." I was referred to work with a couple some years after they had sold their business. Both of them were still very healthy, alert and active. Yet they had some concerns that needed attention. They felt their investment broker wasn't hearing them or was losing direction. They didn't understand their accountant's billing, and also wondered if they needed someone younger. On the legal side, they had re-done wills the year before, but the named executor was admittedly terrible with money and often a threat to family relationships. Three areas of concern!

They were trying to do their own planning since no one else was pulling this together for them. We took these worries off their plate by connecting their advisors as a collaborative team and stewarding their total plan. This couple is confident now that the guidance they are receiving will perpetuate a strong life-income, reduce tax, and sustain desired gifting through their estate.

I'm not saying a person can't be his own lawyer if he's had a career in law. I'm not saying a person can't be her own accountant if she's had a career in accounting. And I'm not saying a person can't DIY with investing if you've had substantial experience in the financial and investment worlds. What I'm sharing is that if you can get professionals in their respective fields to bring their best and collaborate with you as a stewardship team, then your results can far exceed the DIY approach.

5. Fraudulent Advisors

Fraud has damaged and devastated families, charities, pension funds, governments and multinational institutions. The Madoff family is infamous for fraud that "made-off" with billions. Other names appear daily, some listed in Wikipedia at "list of con artists." A related entry on "fraud" is so active that editors are continually updating citations to match current news.

Just as worrisome is the local reach of fraud in one's own community. An Internet search on fraud in any mid-sized town can yield over half a million Web results. Nearby towns offer similar search results. Fraud is in our news every day and seems a perennial part of the human condition.

If your money is important to you, and especially if you're thinking about an amount of money that you might never be able to replace again, then what safety can we find from a world of fraud? How can you lower the chances of fraud happening to you? Here are some considerations that may help.

- Take a personal responsibility and inquisitive interest in how you select an advisor to serve your wealth and wellbeing.

- Has this advisor already proven to be loyal with a lesser sum of money? *Or on the other hand, may you need a higher level of strategy and service?*

- Is the advisor recommended among other peers and professionals? Is she or he known for managing the level of responsibility you will be entrusting?

- Does he or she carry the accreditations that show someone has studied and served with excellence?

- Does this advisor serve under the oversight of duly constituted regulatory authorities?

- Has she or he been subject to penalties for wrongdoing, or is there a clean record of good standing and membership in relevant financial association(s)?

I also personally feel that there is an advantage to having an advisor or advisory firm that never touches your money. If this person is advising on your wealth, let's consider that the institutional platform where your money is invested has distinct and separate fiduciary responsibility. In this event, to move money in, out or within your account, you and your advisor will submit instructions but the advisor never touches the money itself. And the advisor is guiding you based on your written and certified financial planning process. So to me this keeps a safe distinction between the roles of advice and custody, or financial planning and fiduciary care. I appreciate this way of serving my own clients. Furthermore, I've often realized that fraud would be greatly reduced or eliminated if advisors had no access to client monies.

Table for page 96: key value of "income mandates"

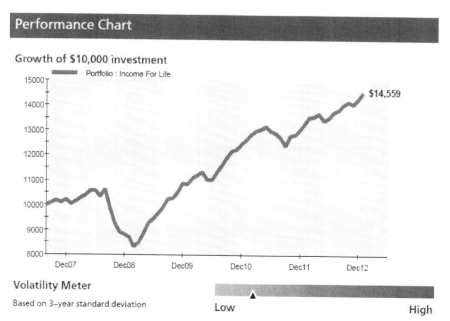

6. Lack of "Life Income Mandates"

I've been developing a thesis over many years to show how people can arrange a strong income for life. Implementing this would be personalized to your own circumstances and investor profile. Let's consider a broad brush-stroke approach of how we may prepare and protect an income for life. If you have five fingers on one hand, consider the following five sources of income and how they can contribute to enjoying your life income. Please also refer to the diagram immediately above on page 95.

Dividends

Dividends are a portion of earnings within corporations that are returned as income to those who are the ultimate owner or beneficiary of such value. Dividend income used to be called "widows and orphans" investments. The reason is clear: strong companies with vigorous mandates, achieving high income and often increasing pay-outs over the years, will help contribute to your income and support your lifestyle. Historically, we might have thought mainly of the larges companies that pay high dividends; today, this is possible also with mid- and smaller-sized companies and representing a variety of industry sectors and regions, thus lowering your risk while helping sustain income for life.

Real Estate

Real estate can be owned personally – we live in real estate – but that's not paying us an income today. Beyond this, there are different types of real estate investment that can support ongoing income: retail, office, industrial, and multi-residential. These may primarily be local or diversified nationally or globally, either as entities on a stock exchange or via a fund directly owning the specific real estate assets. The point is, you want less risk than the stock market while securing an income that will generally rise year-over-year.

Infrastructure

Infrastructure is coming into vogue for similar reasons too. Various countries' national pension plans are being invested in infrastructure. Here it's easy to think of when you last paid a highway toll, or dropped money at a booth while driving over a bridge. Airports, coal and natural gas terminals, even broadband and airwaves (communications) are in this category. Infrastructure development is a key need of emerging countries today, yet also among 'developed nations' whose infrastructure is in massive and immediate need of repair and upgrade. Investors can participate in this area through stocks or the dedicated focus of a fund or pool to diversify your investment. Next time you pay money to use a highway or bridge, or leaving an airport, consider if you'd like to own that type of infrastructure!

Fixed Income

Fixed income products usually refer to cash deposits, bonds, even mortgage securities. The problem today is that interest rates are so low, you could be paid less than inflation – which means your "real return" is actually a loss! There are, however, alternatives. Some developed countries have high debt and low growth rates, while some other countries have lower debt and higher growth rates: I personally feel it sad and misplaced that many people invest in the former without including the latter. We can also find corporations which are bigger than some countries, offering strong cash flow, global enterprise value, and higher coupon rates than many government bonds: yet too often peoples' fixed-income holdings offer little or no corporate exposure. It's clear that your discussion with a qualified advisor is vital to securing the "income" you want to enjoy from fixed-income investments.

Life Payout Annuities

We mentioned the five fingers on a hand, and five ways of contributing to a stable and vital income for life.   The fifth finger here is life payout annuities in order to say they merit examination with someone who is licensed to have this conversation with you. Even if you're too young today to get high income from an annuity, it's worth knowing this kind of instrument can be valuable in future years. Let's say that in our 70s, life annuities can offer a guaranteed foundation of income for life *(...or longer if you elect a guarantee that can outlive you.)*   A life annuity may be especially valuable to someone who had no other pension benefits;

this guaranteed base is combined with other more flexible forms of income. We can also ladder an annuity stream, perhaps at age 72, 75, 78 for example if this fits you. Thus, you've cemented three guaranteed sources of income, each likely higher than before, while dividends and other income sources continue as well. If life payout annuities were to become 10% to 40% of your income, you have this valuable base. You might see it as the legal guarantee that it is impossible for you to ever run out of money.

* **Footnote::** This discussion is not a recommendation of any specific investment or security. Intent here is solely to suggest that in the context of your professional advisory discussions you can seek to identify lower-volatility investment to create and then sustain income over a prolonged period. The graph above on page 95 does not show the impact of withdrawing income during this period, however I've intentionally chosen a most recent and notoriously volatile and negative period of the past two centuries: if this is the litmus test, an "income mandates" approach may win where other designs may fall. Note that only a licensed life insurance advisor can legally discuss and implement Life Pay-out Annuity strategies; also that the p.95 graph does not include income from Life Pay-out Annuity or laddered annuity structures.

7. One Basket Case – and Home Country Bias

Everyone agrees it's unwise to have all your eggs in one basket. Yet very often I find this is a great weakness in peoples' current plans – or rather their lack of financial plans. The goal is to reach both asset- and product-diversification.

A family owns a home, pays down the mortgage religiously, and perhaps is leaving themselves poor outside of the home equity.   If this is their one basket, they'll have difficulty matching their future income needs to this limited basket of wealth.

Some financial advisors have focused only on selling life insurance products. Using that basket exclusively may at some point leave a household short of capital and desperate for income.

Business owners sometimes will stake everything on the future of their business. Some have depleted savings and fully mortgaged their home, their car, even children if they could. But a business is only one basket – hopefully a very strong one – so wouldn't it be vital to know how your other assets relate to this basket and how you will unlock the total picture to create income for your future.

Inheritance or lottery-winnings also can provide one or more baskets. Actually, these sources of money would best be used to help you build a multi-basket approach to safeguard your future.

If you have engaged an accredited financial professional for your planning, you'll find guidance that represents at least five baskets of wealth. Some that would obviously appear in a certified financial plan include:

- Pension values;
- Business values;
- Home and cottage properties;
- Registered investment accounts;
- Non-registered investments;
- Life insurance cash values;
- Living benefit insurances for health & personal care;
- Rental-income properties; and
- Venture capital or Angel investing.

Home country bias is a weakness even if you have the variety of baskets mentioned above. Consider where you live and the values represented today in your home, pension, business, investments, life and health insurances. Reviewing these, would you conclude that 80% to 100% of these are representative of just your own country?

Consider the debt level in our society, and the future health costs that are going to hit our society as the baby boom generation ages. Consider our all-time low interest rates, and what happened in many places to housing values in recent years. What about the red tape and legal burdens on business these days? Would you want all your wealth parked solely within our own country?

The U.S.A. and Euro-zone are each a little more than 21% of the world economy. BRICS (Brazil, Russia, India, China and South Africa) combine at a further 20% of world economy. U.K, Canada and Australia are each within earshot of 3% of world economy. Estimates for the fastest-growing economies of the world, known together as Emerging Markets and Frontier Markets, comprise 35-40% of the world economy.

In many cases, the fastest growing economies have a lower debt burden. Infrastructure development in these economies may have greater immediate leverage than in developed economies. Their currency values may be rising. Their interest rates may be slipping to more favourable levels *(suggesting capital gain on their bonds)*. Ownership, red tape and other legal issues are becoming clearer with time. And when one or a few countries at any point in time have a crisis, the impact on a globally diversified investment plan will be muted. This is safer than what many have experienced since 2008 when investments plummeted, job losses soared, and families were helplessly distressed.

So make this a personal matter. First, think about why you're here: is it about business, pension, inheritance or another significant sum of money in your hands? Then consider the "baskets" that are already represented in your planning, and the approximate exposure you have to fortunes of your home country. What planning or advisory discussions should you have now to protect your wealth and ensure your future income?

8. Missing Life's Horizons: Lack of a Written Financial Plan

I passionately encourage us all to recognize the value and dynamic nature of life's horizons.

Picture this: someone is talking with their advisor about financial planning for retirement and that advisor's computer projects monthly income in a straight or flat line into the future, perhaps with 3% inflation until death. I have to ask: is this realistic?

"Realistic" means real, sensible, practical, the way we live, representing how things are, accurate and true to life. So is a straight line actually realistic? Not a chance. Life will never stay the same. (i) You retire and want to spend more in the early years doing new and wonderful things to fulfill longings and dreams. So the plan for earlier spending may need to be higher than the flat-line approach. (ii) Then time comes to settle and travel less due to general aches and pains, medical events that creep in, and a feeling that time with family is easier than another trip to Tuscany or the Amazon. Life in this mid-period of retirement often costs less and may fall below the flat-line of a software illustration. (iii) Seeing ahead into later years, one or both or you may incur rising costs for personal care. Whether at home or another residence, costs may be higher than ever, far exceeding the flat-line that was assumed years ago.

So we look ahead with what I call **"Horizons Analysis"** as there are generally at least three distinct horizons to a long and rewarding retirement lifestyle:

1. Early years' costs to fulfill your 'bucket-list' of life dreams;

2. Mid-period, we may relax & reduce activities and spending;

3. Later seniority with costs of personal care and comfort.

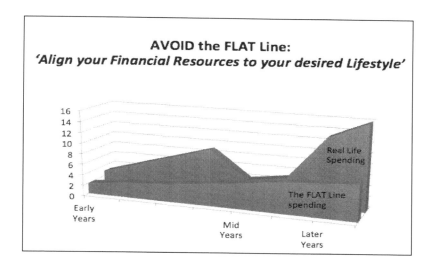

Family needs intersect this too because we don't know when any number of challenges could arise. A daughter suddenly needs help as a single mother. A son at 53 has lost his job with a major international bank and needs financial help getting through the next six months. Or on a happier note, you may choose to invest some money into a business idea for the next generation(s) in your family. That's why we can't trust a computer-generated flat-line. Life is never like that!

Certified planning and preparation for your future can distinguish the assets you own – or need to own – and how they contribute to your future horizons in life. Some assets are probably held in the safety of a designated "income reservoir" to spend in the earliest years enjoying tremendous freedom. Some are safeguarded as a foundation with income and growth for the middle period. Then you have continuing assets with income and growth for later retirement, including insurance that will add to your income when frailty or incapacity arise.

With a plan to embrace such fluctuations in life and spending, you can be confident that your resources will continue to support your retirement and future needs as you choose.

9. Estate Planning by Accident

Here's the picture. A senior fellow is fading away, in the last bed where he'll ever rest, and suddenly he sits bolt upright and exclaims to his family's astonishment: "I've forgotten what I want to be remembered for!"

In another room down the hall is a different scene. This woman worries every day about her family, whether she has done enough, whether she's leaving them safe, if there's something further she could do before she goes. The worry is day and night, a repeating refrain that labours on like her breathing.

Estate planning is an important exercise. But like many kinds of exercise, people often choose to avoid it. The result then is estate planning by accident instead of by design. It's failing to write out a plan. It's not working out ahead of time, not committing to paper, not sharing with family or others, what you most want to have happen when you're gone.

So if you are the person whose health is declining, would you want your estate to be settled without your direct wishes being known? Do you believe your family members all have the same information, and always agree on what you would most value and want? Perhaps so: everyone will know and agree; no one will contest whether you wanted burial or cremation, which gifts you wanted to make and to whom, and how you want certain matters settled or continued once you're gone – right? I mean, in your family, everyone will agree on these things?

Or consider now, you are the spouse, daughter, or son of the person who is dying. Can you confidently say you know all the last wishes of your dear one, and that all your family will also be in total agreement? Can you?

Sadly as you know, there are endless ways that families – good families – can experience conflict at a time of death and bereavement. If it wasn't written down, someone is likely to disagree about something that is done or said. It just happens. It might even result naturally from the fog and confusion of dealing with death itself. And besides this, someone remembers a past conversation, in or out of context, which they feel is a reflection on the deceased's last wishes. Helpful or not, conversations like this arise unless a written plan is in place to comfortably confirm one's last wishes.

Write it down. After thinking of your wishes, discussing them with loved ones, sharing these matters with the closest people in your life, write down your thoughts and wishes. You might include your minister or other faith leader, a funeral planner, or at least someone whom you feel can help put your thoughts effectively into words. An estate lawyer can complete what needs to be put into legal language. And with all this, set a time to share this with your family.

Discussing my clients' legacies and gifts, I suggest the opportunity of leaving a bigger footprint. While in our environmental age we seek a smaller carbon footprint, we might seek a greater testamentary or final footprint. This can include special care in family gifts and community gifting as a continuing of what was already vital to you while you were living. Testamentary trusts and insurance trusts to children and future generations offer an avenue of perpetual memory. Unlimited are the ways your estate planning can seek to remedy child hunger, or eradicate a disease, or enable family and community health, or fund development at a business school, or something related to your faith. It could be northern development or 3rd world development or even the environment.

It's your choice. What do you want to leave as your legacy?

"Let us think like a river, or a waterfall, a cascading flow of nature's goodness and God's blessings, and leave a legacy of beauty and life for all generations to come."

(Echo of environmentalist David Brower, 1912-2000.)

10. Lack of a Stewardship Team

I've spoken earlier of a stewardship team that supports your financial planning. In my world, this involves someone who has at least some form of accredited financial planning designation. It also includes your accounting firm, your legal advisors for business and for your estate, your financial advisors for insurance and investment, perhaps a financial consultant, a business facilitator or whatever your circumstances may require. Overall, your stewardship team will probably comprise at least a few of these positions, along with perhaps a key member of your family as well.

Whoever is on your team and however it is structured, they must have a laser-focus on your key goals and values. What are the results you want? What should you avoid? How should your wealth express your purpose and value as a human being and a member of your family? How will your income support the life you want? Should that income rise with or beyond inflation? How can it be tax-effective? Do you want to include family gifts and charitable giving? How will you provide funding and authority for health decisions and personal care? And how would you be remembered when you're departed? What impact should continue beyond this lifetime?

A stewardship team is the opposite of do-it-yourself. If your business were being litigated, you wouldn't go to court without legal advisors. If your country were at war, you wouldn't go into battle without a fully developed strategic plan. If your body were battling a deadly illness, you wouldn't rely solely on Internet searches or the advice of one doctor, but rather a team of health professionals. And in the battle against financial mistakes and potential losses through the seasons of life, we wouldn't "do it ourselves" bereft of the resources a team can offer.

Life insurance ignored at our peril:

"In this Darwinian survival-of-the-fittest society of ours, with economic turbulent times most likely in the years ahead, those who have patient accessible capital set aside will benefit the most...."

"Banks have immense resources. They have legions of economists, analysts, attorneys, and accountants to help each bank maximize the efficiency and economic output on its money. ...Banks buy (billions) of life insurance (ranging 10% to over 40% of tier 1 assets) because it provides immeasurable economic benefits, financial stability, and safety..."

Barry James Dyke, <u>The Pirates of Manhattan</u>, 2008.

Chapter 6

Conclusion: Wealth can serve the Life you Choose

What is the measure of wealth? Many people automatically answer: "money!" Certainly, money is a key attribute of wealth. That is why in this book we address money you will receive or have received in the broader context of life values and financial security. Whether the money is from a pension, business, inheritance or winnings, the choices you make and the strategies you pursue will make all the difference in protecting your income stream, your financial security and your legacy to your family and others. These decisions are vital for you in the circumstances you face.

We reviewed the central choices you have if you are approaching your retirement years in a **Pension**: to stay in the plan or commute. I trust you have considered many of the factors that go into this decision. All of you as readers face unique individual situations; the decision you make must reflect these particular circumstances. However, knowledge is power. The more informed you are, and the more you can tap into a stewardship team to guide you, the better your decision will be. It's that simple.

For those contemplating selling a **Business**, the rewards – and challenges – are many. The decision to develop a succession plan hinges on many factors, including whether you want the continuing business to remain in the family, go to existing staff, or be sold to an external buyer. How you want to position this change and what you expect from the outcome of the sale is up to you. Reviewing the transition you want in your business, even your life income and estate planning with those serving as your stewardship team, can pay enormous dividends to your future.

Much has been written about **Inheritance** and the massive transfer of billions of dollars from one generation to the next in the coming years and decades. Instead of plying financial products or offering investment strategies, I have taken a different tack to the topic of giving and receiving within families. Inheritance is inextricably linked to values – those who are giving the money have a clear idea of what it means and the legacy they want to provide. Inheritors can respect these values, and ensure that the money is protected and put to the best use.

Many people dream about **Winnings** and sudden wealth events, such as a lottery or unexpected windfall. These dreams can quickly turn to nightmares if you are unprepared. People may get a sudden influx of money and spend it all – and more – over a matter of months or years. They are like a ship without a rudder. To avoid this situation, develop a strategic plan that embraces your personal values and can achieve your short- and long-term plans and the legacy you want to leave.

In all four of these sections, there is an underlying theme – the desire to maximize your financial security and avoid the pain of needless mistakes. In our final section on **Mistakes to Avoid**, we explored the most prevalent traps people fall into when it comes to life income and financial planning. Some of these traps arise from fear; some from the ignorance of "not knowing what we don't know." If you're serious about preserving your life income stream, enjoying the life you want to live and protecting the legacy you want to leave, read carefully through these common mistakes. Actively seek out a trusted stewardship team to guide you in your decisions. The value you'll receive will far exceed the cost.

Wealth is, of course, about more than money. I have met many people who have lots of money and have "dotted their i's and crossed their t's" through a sound financial plan. Yet, they still feel a void in their lives. They seek a purpose, a meaning. Wealth is about values, legacy and how you want to live your life. In the end, wealth comes down to who you are as a whole human being. What is your purpose? What are your values? What is your legacy? In the end, only you can answer these questions. Hopefully, by reading this book you have begun to explore some of these issues as they pertain to your own life. That is why I call it Lifestyle Financial Planning.

This is, to me, a wonderful reward – knowing you are making this material your own. Clearly some areas here will speak more to your individual situation than others. Feel free to share this material with your family, friends, colleagues – anyone can benefit from asking the right questions.

My fervent hope is that that you build on the areas in which you found the most help and insight. These can form the basis of the decisions you make going forward or provide the framework for an advanced discussion with your trusted stewardship team. This is value you own and carry forward when it comes to your financial security and the life you want to live. No one can take this away from you.

If we could miss the gravest errors

that have robbed people of their wealth

and find how to enjoy the strongest results to

perpetuate the wealth we build & receive in life

HOW AWESOME WOULD THAT BE!

BW

APPENDIX:

1st BONUS: BUILDING YOUR FUTURE DREAM

Some may bypass this section because they already have a sense of how they can live a full and rewarding retirement. But what if your future is a blank screen, an empty canvas? What if you have no idea how you'd fill the days and create purpose and enjoyment?

If this is you – or someone you care about – I can briefly introduce a process to help unlock the lifestyle you want to enjoy in retirement. I've called this process visioning. It expands to become a whole-body creative experience to imagine and build the future you choose.

One evening a few years ago, I was in the living room of a couple who had invited me over to discuss their financial planning. Actually, the truth was, "she" had invited me over. "He" was sitting a bit removed from her, cross-legged in the opposite direction as if to show he wasn't interested in any of what we'd be talking about.

So I opened the subject of their planning for the future …what would it look like? And she replied, "that's why you're here; we have no idea!"

In their daily lives, she owned an expanding business and he was an executive in sales for another firm. Their key story about money and wealth went back fifteen years to a time of great hardship in their lives. They had made some bad decisions and worked extremely hard together to pull themselves out of the mess. So their motivation came from the fear of returning to harsh times. Their biggest financial dream was to avoid trouble.

What I did next with this couple could unlock something for you. You're reading this book because you have financial resources, whether from business, pension, or other wealth events in your life. Like the couple I'm mentioning, you have the financial capacity to enjoy a dream ....and yet perhaps you don't know what this dream can be. You don't want to be bored. You don't want to run out of money. You don't want to get ill and old. But for all the things you don't want, surely there is a mighty and compelling dream that can lead you forward into the life you do want – a life of purpose and meaning and creativity, and wonderfully fulfilling experiences.

So here is the first question I asked Bev and Tony: "If you were waking up somewhere in the world today, and just as you're clearing your mind you realize that you're retired and you're in the very best place in the world, exactly where you want to be. Bev and Tony, please tell me, where are you?"

They paused. It was very quiet. Then Bev replied, "Tuscany" and Tony immediately agreed "Tuscany."

"Great", I said. "So you're waking up this morning in Tuscany and I just want to know, is this a place you are renting or do you own it?"

"We own it", Bev replied eagerly.

"Cool", I replied, and I mentioned, "it's very dark in here because you've just awakened; would you go over and open the ...blinds or curtains, or shutters?"

This stumped them for a moment. They had to think of the setting, and visualize what was covering the windows. "Curtains" they both replied together. And I asked, would one of them get up, put something on as they were rather naked (laughter), and go and throw the curtains open wide. They did this, and we celebrated the morning light flooding their room.

So now I asked: "What do you see through the window?" Bev and Tony were both standing here at the window, peering out westward in the early morning light, and told me of the landscape from here to the glimmering azure blue sea. This we enjoyed for a moment until I asked .....

"Does the window open?" They both looked at me silently. Neither of them had the answer, and then Tony said, "yes it opens" so I invited him to "open the window, take a deep breath of this fresh morning air, and just listen; lean out a little and just listen to everything you can hear Tony." Together I could see they were listening. They mentioned hearing a voice laughing nearby. Children in a park nearby were playing football (soccer) shouting energetically at each other. An older woman dressed in black came into view, her shoes sounding a rhythm on the cobble stones.

I asked them to notice too, the gentle breeze coming in on them, and what other things did they notice? Bev was first to smile with the aroma of bread baking nearby. They mentioned the rich scent of a flowering plant growing along the outside wall. Their nostrils flared open to get the full experience. Bev reached out to touch a flower, caressing it in her open palm, truly satisfied with the beauty and joy of this new day.

As they turned back from the window, we imagined ourselves leaving the room, walking down a flight of stairs and out for breakfast followed by a leisurely walk. They described how people were dressed, sounds of the market and the smells of cheese and meats, and succulent fresh fruit in season. They walked by the water and we heard the birds' symphony while soaring freely on the breeze.

For the afternoon, Bev and Tony took me with them for a drive in the country, describing hills, trees, occasional ruins, sheep and other animals along the way, and occasional breath-taking panoramic views. Dinner in the country was a magnificent and authentic meal of pasta and local wine. Under night stars, they drove home again where, glass in hand, Tony and Bev looked out to admire the deep blue infinite horizon where present and future blend in a rich experience of life at its best.

Now, if that's the movie we made in our minds, hit "pause" because we need to leave it and create our own dreams. But realize too, dreams will change! A couple of years later, Bev told me they no longer wanted to own the place in Tuscany. "It's enough to visit", she said, "but there are so many places we want to go. It just makes more sense to rent a place wherever we want to be. And then we can go anywhere!"

For yourself perhaps the following questions could open some avenues for you.

- If you were to wake up tomorrow morning fully retired (at least for a few weeks) and find yourself in the most wonderful place in the world, where would you be? How would it feel? What would you be saying to yourself in those early quiet moments of the new day? What do you most want to enjoy here? What experiences would bring you the joy and satisfaction you want to experience?

- If life were a movie about you, who are the characters and what are the scenes you want to be writing to express your freedom, the fun and exhilaration, friends and family that make this everything it can be for you?

- What resources could you explore to open up new vistas, tastes and wonderful experiences for the future? What would you find on the web, in tourist brochures, from travel agencies, and among friends? Will you find information on ecological and humanitarian tours? Which continents appeal most to you? Which cities or regions in those places do you find most compelling?

- If you think of the landscape, are you drawn more to mountains or to oceans? Animals or vegetation? Music or to foods? Natural life or theatre? City lights or rural quietude? And what languages are perhaps most comfortable – or intriguing – for you?

- If money were no barrier and you could fully design a time to enjoy exactly as you choose, how will you build this dream?

This visioning can be absolutely life-changing. It's a vibrant experience that draws all our senses into a symphony of tastes and colours and experiencing enormous joy. And by doing this – "experiencing the future now" through this process – you soon realize you can continually make it larger and more creative.

"Life is not a race – but indeed a journey. ...
"Take time for yourself – plan for longevity. ...
Bonnie Mohr, in "Living Life"

2nd BONUS: FINANCIAL PLANNING PROCESS

OUR FORMAL PROCESS OF CERTIFIED FINANCIAL PLANNING

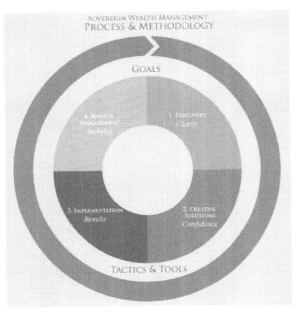

A financial firm you'd trust with your resources and life-goals will describe their process in 4, 5, or 6 stages. Our firm pictures this as a 4-step strategic process in a progressive upward spiral of continuous improvement.

First we establish absolute clarity through discussing and documenting your personal circumstances, needs and goals.

Second we build confidence with powerful and creative solutions arising from all we have learned in the 'discovery' stage and in harmony with your legal and tax planning.

Third we complete a personalized financial plan that specifies what you and we will implement through investments, insurances, and all aspects of your wider planning for life, wealth, and future estate.

Fourth we continue to monitor and manage results through seasons and years to align with your most valued goals and our combined success along the way.

EXPERIENTIAL PROCESS: AS CLIENTS DESCRIBED MY PROCESS

Aligning Financial Resources with Life Goals

Choose your dreams – identifies key values for you in money & life; goals for lifestyle, retirement, and future estate.

Capture your dreams – establishes our financial strategies to achieve and secure goals for life & wealth, as documented in your certified financial plan and aligning with legal and tax advisors.

Cherish your dreams – represents ongoing assessment and updating of your financial process to adjust as your personal needs or outside circumstances change along the way.

Create bigger dreams – suggests people can live larger and more abundantly as their income- and financial planning provides significant gifting for family and wider community. I call this "leaving a bigger footprint" as our impact for life and loved ones can successfully live beyond us.

As mentioned on the prior page, financial planning is a formal process of 4, 5, or 6 steps. Many may experience this less formally as an organic and progressive story of how they live life.   The design above captures how clients described my process and the results we achieve for their life-long security, confidence, and loved ones.

3rd BONUS: 20 ways to Brainstorm your future:

Three new experiences you want to enjoy

Three new places you would like to travel

Three conversations to have with your spouse

Three things you can do to help the environment

Three activities to help others in your community

Three people you can speak with to get new ideas

Three reasons you want to enjoy life to its fullest

Three 'chores' you might start enjoying in retirement

Three skills you might use for charitable purposes

Three games that sharpen/stimulate mental focus

Three ways you'll keep healthy in spring/summer

Three ways you'll keep healthy in autumn/winter

Three hobbies you already enjoy (or can learn)

Three great events that bring your family together

Three ways to keep family contact when traveling

Three friends (or groups) you want to keep forever

Three ways that faith/spirituality guides your future

Three ways faith/spirituality allows you to help others

Three reasons for gratitude each morning and evening

Three ways to expand this brainstorming to new levels...

Index

At least 20% of the proceeds of this book will assist:

The Early and Lifelong Nutrition Fund

hosted in the Oakville Community Foundation (Ontario)

and in the Burlington Community Foundation (Ontario)

And also the

Indigenous Sharing and Learning Centre

at Laurentian University, Sudbury, Ontario

And other human relief and development services globally.

Thank you for your support to help expand resources

for stronger homes, futures, communities, and world!

Yours gratefully,

Brian Weatherdon

20860126R00073

Made in the USA
Charleston, SC
30 July 2013